'You've always known I was a pornographer,' said my mother. 'That's what I do.'

'But why?' I asked. 'Why write things you won't let us read?'

'I've told you lots of times,' said my mother. 'People need something to take their minds off how lousy their lives are. If they weren't provided with illicit pleasures, they'd just invent them for themselves. And whatever they come up with would probably be a lot more anti-social than Arkism.'

'But you always say that pornography demeans people,' I said. 'And exploits them. So how can you stand writing it?'

My mother looked at me sadly.

'It's all I can do,' she said finally.

Greg Michaelson works and lives in Edinburgh.

the wave singer

Greg Michaelson

ARGYLL✠PUBLISHING

© Greg Michaelson 2008

First published in 2008 by
Argyll Publishing
Glendaruel
Argyll PA22 3AE
Scotland
www.argyllpublishing.com
www.thewavesinger.co.uk

The author has asserted his moral rights.

British Library Cataloguing-in-Publication Data.
A catalogue record for this book is available from
the British Library.

ISBN 978 1 906134 27 3

Printing: Athenaeum Press, Gateshead

Contents

To be homeless is to be nameless.

Outside

1 My mother was a pornographer. The best in the business, my father said. He'd been confined to a wheelchair since his fall from the high tower. Every morning, he made us breakfast and took us to the Village school. My mother rose early and left the house before we were up. Once in late Spring, roused by the swallows under the eaves, I watched her from the loft window, small in her broad black cape, leather case under her arm. In the long winter evenings, after the candles had burnt down, we could see the flickering rush light from under her studio door. Don't disturb your mother, my father would caution with pride. My father had been the head tailor on the number three sail; his life's work. Every last stitch tight and true, he told us. Now he stayed at home, cooking and cleaning, cajoling and comforting. Not that my mother was distant. Perhaps a little aloof. But that was her calling.

The Village stood amongst the rice paddies. Stone and wood. Snug in the snow if sultry in summer. Every Thursday, the barge brought fresh supplies for the Store and took away the great hessian sacks of cereal. If someone in the Town had remembered, there'd be a film for the hall. Then the next Sunday evening, the caretaker would carefully top up the projector with oil and the whole Village would gather round the screen. Sometimes there were fresh books for the library. There were rumours that there were books in the Fort. Not the sort of books you wanted to read, my father said.

My mother worked in the Fort. Every morning she cycled along the boardwalk, snaking amongst the water beds, that joined our Village to the Promontory. Once a year, my school gave a concert in the Fort. Once a year, one of us was chosen to become a Wave Singer. Wave Singers sang on the important days in the year. At the Equinoxes and Solstices. On Kropotkin's birthday. Wave Singers sang at the Spring tide, high on the dyke, while the great wooden flood gates were winched into place. The song of the Wave Singers, my father would say, is the most beautiful song that you ever can hear. Remember each one. Remember where you were when you heard it. One day someone may ask you. Poppycock, said my mother, plaiting paper clips into his long brown pigtails.

I'd been taken to every Singing since I'd been born. Eight a year. Always on the same days. Of course I can't remember them all. But he could. My father said that you knew when people were born and when people died by the Singings. You knew when to plant the rice and when to crop it. You measured the sail by the Singings. You'll not be measuring sails again, said my mother, shuddering.

My father was an Arkist. Every morning, after he'd taken us to school, he sat with his friends folding rice leaves into Arkles, tiny green simulacra of the Ark. The Ark was enormous, big enough to hold the whole Village and all the animals. From a distance, the Ark looked like all the other Arks; a huge, squat hull. Close up, it seemed improbable that the Ark could ever float. Even though the original wooden shell had long been layered in sheets of scrap metal, scavenged from the ruins beyond the Fort, the yellow light from the Arkists' tallow candles still seeped between the seams. My father said that if you folded one million Arkles and put them inside the Ark, that would be enough to keep you afloat when the Great Flood came. Fiddlesticks, said my mother, putting another peat into the pot-bellied stove. When the Great Flood comes we'll all drown. You'll see.

Many of the Arkists were former Wave Singers. Every year, at the concert in the Fort, the oldest Wave Singer would select someone to replace them. The new Wave Singer went to live in the Fort as the oldest Wave Singer's apprentice. Once they had passed on all of their Songs, the oldest Wave Singer left the Fort and returned to the Village. The Villagers were welcoming. Wave Singing was our highest calling. But the Wave Singers could only hear the Waves. Younger children were a bit frightened of the Wave Singers and tended to avoid them. They did seem a bit strange, said my father. When you talked to them, somehow they were never quite there. But they made perfect Arkles that were always the same size and shape. What an abject waste of time, said my mother scornfully. Arkles don't grow on trees, my father would say. There aren't any trees, said my mother, stirring the custard.

During the monsoon, my father complained of his arthritis, saying that his fingers were so stiff that he couldn't manipulate the rice leaves. He would look hopefully at my mother and ask her if she could spare some paper to tear into soft strips. And what would I write on, said my mother.

When she wasn't working, my mother liked to read, even though she spent most of her waking hours writing for others, lost in worlds of her own imaginings. Given half a chance she'd read all the books in the library, my father would say. My mother thought that words were just about all that mattered. She'd taught us all to read before we could walk and always brought us back books from her mid-Singings trips to the Town. But when we asked if we could read what she wrote, she'd look cross. There are lots of books here, she said. Have you finished them all yet? My father said that our house would fall down if you took all the books away. Every wall in every room was shelved from floor to ceiling. Every surface had books on it.

Every Spring Singing, my mother reorganised all of the books. Under her direction, we'd take them off the shelves and make great piles in the yard. My mother then looked at each book in turn, telling us where to replace it, according to some scheme known only to herself. Rarely, she'd hand a book to my father to put into the recycling box. We all knew that, after we'd gone to bed, she'd have second thoughts and forgive the outcasts. You love your books more than you love us, my father would complain. Balderdash, said my mother, stroking his ginger sideburns. Anyway, they're our books not my books.

Of course we hadn't finished all the books in the house. But most of them weren't the sort of books we wanted to read. We liked books about why things are the way they are; books about how things work and how to make things; books about plants and animals; books about other places and other peoples; books about the past and the future; books about the soil and the sea and the stars and the seasons. But my mother's books were full of adjectives and adverbs. We didn't care for modifiers. We liked practical books. Only children read stories.

I liked going to choir practice and especially enjoyed singing shanties, rounds and fugues. I wasn't so fond of the Song. In choral singing, you sing with each other. There's a small number of distinct, well defined, complementary parts that set each other off. As you sing your own part you can hear all the other people singing the same part around you. You can also hear all the other parts and the more you practise together, the more you can let go.

Singing a Song is altogether different. You stand in a Strand, making the shape of the Song. Its impossible just to Sing with your brain floating free. You have to become one with the Song, focusing carefully on the rest of Strand, especially on the Singers on either side of you. How they Sing intimately affects how you Sing and how you Sing affects them in turn. Its said that the two End Singers have the hardest parts, but its actually much easier only having to reflect one other voice.

As a child you start with simple Corner Songs – dodecahedrons, octagons, hexagons, pentagons, squares and finally triangles— gently acquiring the elementary Waves. Initially, all Corners sing the same Wave together, with no sense of Time or Place. Then each Corner takes it in turns to Sing against the others, moving their Waves ever so slightly in and out of Phase. Slowly you learn how to listen to and respond to your nearest Corners.

Next you move onto the Island Song, with its endless, circular Strand. You need to acquire a sense of the whole Song, of the Waves rippling round and round. You start to read the Song notation, learning how the Waves form more complex Breakers, depending on the Rocks and the Winds and the Tides. Finally you split the Island into a linear Strand and start to practise the Village Song for the Neap Tide Singing in the Fort.

When they're young, everyone eventually learns their entire Village Song. It's said that, before, Stretches used to be fixed in length, passing from mother to eldest son and father to eldest daughter. Now, each year, you're given a random Stretch of Strand depending on how many are in the choir. My father said that so long as everyone can sing any Stretch then the Strands can never be lost. Some households Sing together but not ours. My father loves the Songs but has perfect pitch. My mother has an astonishing voice but only Sings rarely. She'd been chosen as a child but had refused. Such a shame, my father would say. Such an escape, said my mother.

Actually, steel recordings of all of the original Songs were held in the Fort. Sometimes our choir teacher would borrow our Village Song and the caretaker would bring the record player up from under the stage. The recordings had been made long before the waters receded and our peoples fled from the barren lands onto the fertile sea beds. We always listened in silence even though we all knew every last whisper of the long lost sound of our shores.

When we first began to Sing, we wanted to hear our Song over and over again, to learn it by rote, but our choir teacher said that the recording was just a frozen sequence in time and space. We shouldn't listen to the recording as a Song in itself but as a ghost for our Singing to fit round. A Song wasn't so much a single sequence of sounds as a family of sequences, all closely related but still all slightly different. A Song had unchanging elements: the camber of the strand; the texture of the sea bed; the positions of the rocks and inlets. These all defined the underlying shape of the Song. But the Song changed with the time of day and the time of year, with the wind and the tide and the rain.

My mother and father's greatest pleasure was taking baths. It was understood that any of us could have showers whenever we liked but that baths were special. Once a month, my father would stoke the pot bellied stove. When the bathroom had filled up with all of our water, my mother would heave my father up the ladder and shut the hatch behind them. When they emerged several hours later, pink and sated, the rest of us would take it in turns to pump the grey soapy water through the filters and back into the huge tank under our house.

In the books my mother read, people liked to sing in the bath. My father said that singing was the last thing he wanted to do in his bath. There's singing and singing, said my mother, darkly. It was said that the Wave Singers in the Fort could have baths whenever they liked. It was said that the Wave Singers always ate well. It was said the Wave Singers could read the books my mother wrote.

For about a month before the last Spring Singing, the sky had been full of clouds. We were used to Spring clouds. They were wispy white, ethereal, translucent. They never rained. They just drifted slowly away. These clouds were different. They were dark and dense, casting deeper shadows than the monsoon clouds of late summer.

The morning of the last Spring Singing, we carried all the books outside, and laid them out in rows corresponding to the rooms and shelves that housed them. My mother walked briskly along each line, passing books back to my father who followed her with a box on his knees. When each box was full, one of us would carry it back indoors and carefully replace its contents according to my mother's current taxonomy.

As my father handed me a box of those tedious tales my mother said were known as Airport Novels, I slipped and the books went flying. My mother sighed and bent down to retrieve them. One had landed spine up, pages akimbo. As she straightened the leaves, she turned angrily towards us. Who did this, she shouted. Look, the last ten pages are missing. She picked up another book and inspected it. This one's the same, she cried. Come on. Who did this. She checked all of the books from the box. They all lacked the last ten pages.

My mother sat down amongst her mutilated books, held her head in her hands and rocked slowly backwards and forwards, keening sorrowfully. We tried to comfort her but she gently pushed us away. We turned anxiously to my father. My father looked broken.

There was a low, diffuse rumbling from all around, the sky suddenly darkened, and it began to rain. Quick, said my mother, pulling herself together, we must save them. She gathered up an armful of books and rushed into the house. My father told us to fill the boxes and pile them up on his lap. We took it in turns to push him back across the yard and deposit the books in the hall. Most had escaped with damp covers. Inside the house, my mother carefully wiped each one down and replaced it on its shelf.

Lunch was uncharacteristically sombre. My father had prepared a fine spread from the kitchen garden but nobody felt like eating. I noticed that, whenever my mother said anything to him, he didn't meet her eye. After lunch, my mother returned to the shelves and inspected each book, frequently muttering to herself. Here's another. And another.

The rain fell steadily and the water level in the paddy fields slowly rose. By mid afternoon it was lapping over the boardwalk to the Fort. My father, fearful of the Great Flood, said that we should board the Ark. Don't be absurd, said my mother, fiercely. We're going to the Singing, just as we always do. We put on our best clothes, unfurled our umbrellas and walked to the Fort. My mother strode ahead, wrapped in her cape, hugging her leather bag. My father wheeled himself along behind, anxiously checking the sky.

The Fort stood on the Promontory jutting out into the Channel. The closely packed rectangular stone buildings were enclosed by high, angled ramparts. At the eastern end, a rusty barbed wire fence stopped anyone from venturing into the poisoned waste beyond. The boardwalk ended at the foot of the broad steps that led up to the top of the northern ramparts and into the Fort.

The dyke ran across the Channel from the tip of the western-most rampart to the Point on the opposite shore. The rain fell in torrents, harder and harder. My father urged us to abandon the Singing and get into the Ark. We'll do no such thing, said my mother. We carried him up the steps, and walked out onto the ramparts and along the dyke.

At the South Gate, we joined our neighbours. On the far side of the North Gate, we could see our friends from the next Village. On the platform above the Gates, the Wave Singers had formed the opposing convex Strands of the Promontory and the Point. At the first signal from the Gatekeepers, we took up our stations at the windlass; the youngest nearest the centre and the eldest at the ends of the levers. My mother carefully put her leather bag down where she could keep an eye on it.

Once my mother forgot her leather bag and my father asked me to take it to her. Halfway along the boardwalk, I stopped and opened it, and furtively browsed the book she was currently writing. It was really quite shocking; full of people who wouldn't work, who seemed to spend their lives talking to each other and consuming enormous quantities of food. It wasn't clear where the food came from or who grew and prepared it. Certainly, the people in the story didn't. They never seemed to finish their meals but it wasn't clear what happened to all the leftovers. Given how hard and yet how pleasant our lives are, I blushed to think that anyone could enjoy reading about such idleness and waste. Shamefaced, I put the book back in the bag and delivered it to my mother.

At the second signal from the Gatekeepers, the Wave Singers began to Sing. Although we could barely hear them above the noise of the rain, we walked slowly round and round, winding the coarse hempen ropes onto the capstan, hauling the South Gate into the Channel to meet its sibling.

As the Wave Singers approached the Song's crescendo, a huge wall of water raced down the Channel and smashed the Gates aside. We all rushed to the edge of the dyke. Our fields had long disappeared and the water rose steadily over the houses. My poor books, said my mother sadly. Well, at least we're all still alive.

At first the Ark rose with the water. My father, peevish, told us that we should have gone there while we still had time. But as the Ark strained against its moorings, it began to break up, and hundreds and thousands of Arkles floated across the flood plain. My mother peered at them. White Arkles, she said. My pages. She wept quietly. My father reached up and hugged her.

2 We spent the night in the Fort. We all knew where to sleep. The whole Village practised evacuation every year. There was lots of rice and dried beans and maize in the Fort, and fresh water from the deep well. Our household had eight bunk berths in the basement dormitory. My mother took the blankets out of our locker and we made up the beds. I slept on the top bunk nearest the corner.

The next morning, the flood had subsided. The sky was still dark but the wind had changed. After breakfast in the great stone dining hall, we made our way back down the rampart steps and along the boardwalk to the Village. Many of the animals had drowned and the paddies were full of salt water. Everything was sodden and covered in a thin layer of mud. My father had brought kindling from the Fort. While my mother grimly inspected the shelves, we wiped down the stove and laid a fire. Our stores were dry in their tightly stoppered jars. Once the fire had caught, my father made tortillas on the hot plate and sent us off to gather peats.

It was a good three hours walk to our stretch of moor. We didn't like to spend much time on the land. We kept to the beach and followed the shore line most of the way. Debris from the flood littered the plain. In the small cove, I picked up and unwrapped a white Arkle. It was the denouement from one of my mother's favourite novels: the heroine, who misunderstood the hero's apparent disinterest, finally discovers that he secretly loves her and is now free to marry her, having cleared his family's falsely besmirched name. Until that day, I had thought my father a guileless man.

We climbed the path through the dunes onto the moor. The wet heather was springy under foot. Many years ago the moor had been a battlefield. We all knew the story of the Prince who wanted to be King. Sometimes, cutting peats, our spades would uncover bones. We often found musket balls. The lead was pure and could be recast.

We filled our sacks with dry peats from the bottom of the pile. Then we sat down and ate our lunch. It was midday and the wind had dropped. From high on the moor we could see clear across the Firth to the shores beyond.

Smoke rose from the Colony on the far side of the moor. The Colonists lived a meagre life. Their soil was thin and their burn often ran dry. We kept pigs and chickens and ducks. The Colonists hunted the feral sheep on the moor. We gave them rice and eggs and bacon in return for their coarse homespun cloth.

The Colonists distilled spirits from fermented rice. I had read that engines could be fuelled by alcohol and wondered why we didn't use them. My father told us that our population was too small to support production on a big enough scale. He said that the sake was only for medicinal purposes: it eased his rheumatism during the monsoon. Havers, said my mother, taking a long pull from her glass.

We finished our tortillas, shouldered our sacks and started back down the dunes.

The sacks were heavy and we were tired. About halfway down, a rabbit ran across my path. I started and fell heavily onto my left leg. The bone poked white through the rip in my trousers. It didn't hurt much. My siblings did their best to make me comfortable and went back to the Village for help.

I was propped up against a dune. I was quite low down and I

couldn't see very much. Everything was quiet. I knew it would take them six hours to get back but I wasn't really frightened. I'd spent nights alone on the dunes before. Just a bit anxious. My leg began to hurt. I hoped there weren't any sheep near by.

To keep myself company, I started to Sing a dodecahedron Corner Song based on my Neap Tide Stretch. I was on the seventh Corner when a voice joined mine, raw but fresh. A young woman appeared over the dune. She had crazed red hair and large feet. She stopped and looked down at me.

'Where are you from?' she asked.

'The Village,' I said.

'I thought so,' she said. 'You Villagers don't much like it up here, do you.'

'No,' I said.

'Are you hurt?' she said.

'Yes,' I said. 'My leg's broken.'

'Wait here,' she said, and disappeared into the dunes.

We didn't have much to do with the Colonists. We found them too abrupt. They rarely came to our Village. They thought us weak and complacent. We met at the monthly markets in the Fort. My father said that the Colonists were all crackpots. They're misguided but they mean well, said my mother, washing his feet.

The pain in my leg increased. I felt cold and despondent. I began to sing again.

I was on the ninth Corner when the girl returned with a man and a woman. The man carried a furled stretcher. The woman bent over and inspected my leg.

'We can't do anything here,' she said.

They carefully lifted me onto a stretcher and carried me across the moor. Nobody said anything. With every jolt my leg throbbed.

I'd never been to the Colony before. As we came near, we passed mounds of eviscerated household goods from before the Event. The Colonists craved electricity. The Store in Town was full of old refrigerators and washing machines and tumble driers and dish washers. The Colonists extracted their motors and constructed ingenious devices to turn them; windmills, water races and treadmills, all linked to a primitive grid. But with no reliable source of motive power and no means to store electricity, the Colonists could not sustain an uninterrupted supply.

The Colony consisted of a large circle of low stone and wooden huts, much like those in our Village, enclosing an open grassy area full of empty barbed wire pens. There was no Ark. It was late afternoon and getting dark. I was carried into a rectangular building. They put the stretcher on a long, low table in the centre of the room.

'We'll need more light,' said the man to the girl.

She mounted the exercise bicycle and started to pedal. The building's rafters were woven with threads of tiny bulbs which swelled into life. I'd never seen electric light before. It was quite unlike the illumination from our candles and oil lamps. So clear and diffuse. No flicker. No smoke. No sharp shadows.

The man cut away my trouser leg.

'It's a clean break,' said the woman. 'But its going to hurt a lot. We can give you something to take your mind off it.'

She took a corked glass bottle from the shelf behind her, poured a large draught of a dark green liquid into a cup and offered it to me.

'What is it?' I asked.
'Hemp tincture,' she said.

I carefully lent onto one side, took the cup and sipped gingerly. The tincture tasted foul.

'Drink it down,' said the woman. 'She can't keep cycling for ever.'

I quickly drained the cup.

'I'm going to straighten your leg,' said the woman. 'Then I'll set the bone and strap you up. Does anyone know you're here?'

'My brother and sister went for help,' I said, 'but they probably think I'm still in the dunes.'

'We'll send a message if we don't hear from them,' said the woman.

'Lie back now,' said the man, pushing me gently down onto the table.

A feeling of warmth slowly suffused my chest. Above me, the myriad lights surged rhythmically with the girl's pedaling. Deep inside I could feel my Corner Song, rippling round in time to the lights. My leg eased as I focused on the Song.

Suddenly, the man pinned me firmly by the shoulders, the woman took my leg, there was an unbearably sharp pain and I passed out.

When I came to I felt confused and thirsty. There was a dull ache from my leg. The sun was up and I was lying on my back, on a palliasse on the floor, covered in a grey blanket. The girl sat at the table watching me, her red hair haloed in the shaft of light from the open door.

'You don't half snore,' she said. 'Would you like something to eat?'

'Something to drink please,' I said.

She helped me into a sitting position against the wall and rolled back the blanket. My leg was wrapped tightly in woollen bandages, sandwiched between two splints. She poured me a cup of water and passed it to me. The water was flecked brown and tasted slightly peaty.

'Don't worry,' she said. 'We boil all the water.'

'Thank you for helping me,' I said. 'What's your name?'

'We don't use names,' she said.

'How do you know who you're talking about?' I asked.

'It's obvious,' said the girl. 'Are you hungry?'

I nodded. She passed me a plate of rice cakes and an apple. We didn't eat many apples. The Colonists grew crisp, sweet ones.

I was finishing the last rice cake when a red-headed boy put his head round the door.

'Are you coming?' he said.

'I'll be right along,' said the girl.

'What about me?' I asked, as she helped me ease back down onto the bed.

'I'll see you in a while,' she said. She topped up the cup with water, covered me with the blanket and left.

I looked around the room. It was painted white and floored with sheepskin rugs. The end wall was shelved with clocks. They all showed different times. Each clock's tick was sharp and angular. Each clock's tick was slightly out of beat with the others, like the manic Song of some concrete coastline.

I dozed fitfully and had strange, urgent dreams. I was standing high on the dunes looking out over the sea that filled our Village's broad flat valley. Every time I moved, pain shot through my leg. The sea was alive with my Stretch. I was far too hot and soon finished the water. I Sang with the sea and the sea Sang with me. When the girl returned, I was soaked in sweat and my bladder was bursting.

'How are you doing?' she asked.

'I feel really lousy,' I said.

'We're going to take you home,' she said. 'They'll meet us on the shore.'

'How will I get there?' I asked. 'I can't possibly walk.'

The girl gave me another draught of the tincture. Then she went outside and fetched a dilapidated red metal trolley. She folded up the blanket and laid it down on the flat-bed.

'On you get,' she said.

She helped me onto the trolley and handed me a pair of wooden crutches. Then she trundled me out of the building and along the dirt track that crossed the green. Three pens now held sheep, bleating lustily. As we left the green and passed the last hut, I asked the girl to stop.

'What for?' she said, stopping.

'I really need to pee,' I said.

She hauled me up onto the crutches. I stood there, wobbling, balanced on my right leg, not knowing what to do. She undid my trouser buttons and took the right hand crutch from me. When I'd finished, she buttoned me up and sat me down again. I still blushed pink as we left the Colony.

'Where are we going?' I asked.

'You'll see,' she said.

The dirt track cut a straight line through the heather, towards the coast but away from our peats. The girl, silent, pulled me along behind her. Our Village is driven by gossip: other people are far more interesting than novels. I wasn't used to being quiet in company, especially when there were so many things to find out about. I was particularly puzzled by her complete lack of interest in me, given how much she was helping me.

'How did you know my Song?' I asked.

'I listened to you,' she said.

'Do you have your own Song?' I asked.

'Our songs aren't like yours,' she said, and began to sing.

Six silver balls in the setting sun.

Of course she sang about the Event. We all learnt about the Event at school. After the fossil fuel ran out, six satellites were launched to convert sunlight into micro-wave radiation, and to beam it back to ground stations at the poles and on the equator. When one satellite was in the earth's shadow, the others could divert energy to it, to maintain the supply below.

Five of them fell and that left just one.

After huge solar flares, five of the satellites failed simultaneously. Instead of sending their energy back to earth, they routed it to the sixth in the earth's shadow.

The last one fired with a roaring crash.

Before it disintegrated, the sixth satellite dumped a vast bolt of radiation onto the Pacific station, vaporising the receiver and the island and millions of litres of surrounding sea water.

The earth went tilt and the sea went smash.

More water poured into the void, knocking the earth off balance. The shock destroyed almost all human habitation and set up enormous, slow, standing waves in the oceans. It was one of the smaller waves that swept across our Village two days ago. My father said that when all the standing waves coincided, the Great

Flood would come. My mother said nothing.

The track began to slope gently up hill and the girl stopped singing.

'Why do you have so many clocks?' I asked.

'To tell the time,' she said, patiently.

'But none of them agree,' I said.

'They're mostly right on average,' she said. 'I reset them every month or so.'

A latticed wooden structure came into view. When we reached the frame, the girl pulled the trolley onto a landing stage that jutted out over the cliff. Then she walked to the end of the stage, leaned over and shouted: 'We're ready!'.

A rope ran in from the cliff, through a series of pulleys around the frame and back out again. Above me, a webbing sling hung from one side of the rope. The girl pulled the sling down behind me and eased me into it.

'Good bye,' she said.

She went to the rear of the frame and began to crank a handle. I was pulled slowly off the trolley and, suspended in mid-air, descended the cliff towards a second frame on the shore. Half way down, I passed another sling carrying the red-headed boy back up. He smiled at me and waved.

3 My brother and sister were waiting for me at the lower frame with my father's best wheelchair. As they took it in turns to push me back to the Village, they told me how they'd gone for help but had decided that they had little prospect of finding me after the sun went down. Leaving early that morning, they'd met up with the red-headed boy who had shown them the way to the hoist.

We went back along the path between the dunes and our fields. The fields were full of people, flushing out the salt water along the irrigation ditches with fresh water from the canal. They raised and lowered the sluice gates by hand, alternately flooding and emptying each paddy in turn. It struck me that the Colonists would have built pumps, or found some other mechanical means to control the gates. My sister and brother were fascinated by the Colonists and asked me incessantly about my brief stay with them. Normally, I would have delighted in describing what had happened to me. On that day I found their questions tiresome.

I was worn out by the time we got home. My father was fretting in his second best wheelchair. My mother had gone to work as usual. I went to bed for the rest of the day. I felt listless and displaced. I was used to routine, to predictability. I was also used to talking through every activity before starting it, while doing it and after it was over. The Colonists just seemed to know what to do and got on with it.

Why did such calm and efficient people waste so much time on machines? They could use a sun dial or an hour candle to tell the time. And they could have lit lamps to mend my leg. Why hadn't they just carried me back down the dunes? Yet the electric light had been so pure and bright. And the ticking of the clocks had sung to me of a different way of ordering the world.

When my mother came home, she undid the straps and inspected my leg. It was bruised purple and blue, and there was a neat row of stitches along the angry red gash where the bone had poked through. My father fussed from the corner. He was worried that the wound might be infected or that the bone might set crooked. They've done a good job, said my mother, swabbing my leg down with rice spirit and binding me up again. I told her about the tincture and my strange dreams. It's been a long time since I've had any, said my mother, wistfully.

I spent most of the next six weeks at home. It was very dull. My father bustled about, cooking the meals, dreaming of the wind in the high tower, organising the washing, singing sad songs of love and loss, keeping a weather eye on all of us. My class teacher visited me every day, bringing me texts to read and problems to solve. Once a week the choir came to rehearse in our house. Meanwhile my mother went silently between the house and the Fort. The shelves were bare. We sensed something boiling up inside her.

One evening, my mother inspected my wound and pronounced me healed. Then she told us that she was going to the Town on the next barge. She needed to visit the Store. The barge left in two day's time. She asked me if I wanted to go with her.

I was very excited. My cousins lived in the Town, with my mother's brother, Rufus. I hadn't been there for over two years. Rufus had been chief engineer on the Bootstrapping. The last time I went was just after Sally's burial. Rufus introduced my parents to each other. Sally was my cousins' mother. My father spoke up for Rufus when the Bootstrapping failed and he lost the use of his legs. Sally took a cold that winter and never shook it off.

My father sent my brother and sister off to collect more peat. I limped along behind them, leaning on a stick. The fields were being replanted with rice. My legs felt stiff and achy as we climbed the dunes. Once we were at our diggings, I sat on a stack of peat while they filled their sacks. I Sang to myself but there was no reply.

Looking across the moor, I saw the girl and boy in the clearing at the Colony's entrance. Behind them a group of people was hammering something together. The girl was flying a kite. The boy was sitting at a table.

I walked slowly over to join them. The boy was bent over a clockwork radio. A wire from the kite ran to the radio. As the boy slowly turned the tuning knob, a uniform faint hiss came from the speaker.

'What are you up to?' I asked.
'Listening,' he said, looking up.
'What are you listening for?' I asked.
'Others,' said the boy.
'There aren't any Others,' I said.
'How do you know?' said the boy.
'Have you ever heard any?' I asked.
'We're not sure,' said the boy.

My mother told us bedtime stories about Others. There were Others who crossed the oceans in a nuclear submarine looking for survivors; Others in black-shrouded sailing ships who plundered quiet settlements like ours; Others in space, clinically taking notes, hatching devious plans to conquer our quiescent planet. My father said that there were no Others. If there were we'd have heard from them by now. There was only us.

'What are they making?' I asked, pointing towards the group constructing what looked like a children's roundabout out of wood and iron.

'It's the new power unit,' said the girl, anchoring the kite string to a stout wooden stake.

'You don't have enough people to keep it turning,' said I.

'We won't need to,' said the girl.

'How will you drive it then?' said I.

'Sheep,' said the boy.

'You'll not get sheep to turn that wheel,' said I.

'Why not?' said the boy. 'They used to be domesticated.'

My siblings called to me. As I reluctantly turned to rejoin them, the hiss from the speaker changed to staccato bursts of high pitched trilling.

'Time?' said the girl, unfolding a grubby piece of paper divided into finely ruled columns of dates and numbers.

'12.43,' said the boy.

'Setting?' said the girl.

'98.4,' said the boy.

The girl wrote down the numbers. The chirping died and the hiss returned.

'What was that?' I asked.

'We don't know,' said the boy.

'You must have some idea what it is,' I said.

'Well we don't,' said the boy.

'Do you hear it often?' I asked.

'Most days,' said the girl.

'Is there any pattern?' I asked.

'We usually pick it up between eleven in the morning and one in the afternoon,' said the girl, 'but we can't spot any regularity to the time or frequency. It never lasts more than a few seconds'

'How long have you heard it for?' I asked.

'There are records going back years,' said the boy.

My siblings were shouting and waving frantically. They were anxious to go but didn't want to leave me behind. I hobbled back across the moor, shouldered a small bag of peat and followed them.

The sound I'd heard on the radio had an urgency about it, as if demanding a reply. It was much livelier than a shelf full of clocks, but far more mechanical than a Strand of Singers. We were taught at school that it was just conceivable that there were other self sustaining communities like the peoples of the Glen, but that there was no practical way of locating them. It seemed implausible that any could have recovered sufficiently to produce enough electricity for communication, given the failure of our own Bootstrapping.

I told my parents about my second encounter with the Colonists. My father said that, for many years after the Event, people had scanned the radio waves, hoping for signs of life. Nothing had ever been heard. The noise from the radio was probably caused by something going wrong inside it. My father said that some people hadn't been able to accept the decision to abandon attempts to locate other groups and to produce electricity. That was why they'd moved to the Colony. But we were alone in the universe and our only hope of survival was the Ark.

My mother, whom I increasingly suspected of a certain degree of dissimulation, sat silently throughout my father's diatribe. Normally she was quick to counter what she called his archaisms. I couldn't tell if she was hiding something from us or, worn out by the loss of her books, could no longer be bothered.

The next morning after breakfast, I packed a small sack, and we all walked to the basin. My mother, dressed as usual in her black cape, carried a large but almost empty sack and her leather bag. At the jetty, we said our farewells and boarded the barge. The bargees had already loaded the hold. The barge master cast off from the jetty and the east wind caught the single square rigged sail. I was very relieved. If the wind changed or dropped we would have to take it in turns to row.

We sat with the other passengers under the awning on the flat rear deck. The canal led through our fields to the mouth of the Glen between the Mountains. The barge entered the lock which slowly filled with water, lifting it to the level of the Loch that ran the length of the Glen. When we left the lock, we kept close to shore, following the west bank. The heather on the mountain flanks glowed purple in the rising sun. Every so often, we passed the tumbled shell of a stedding, overgrown with bushes. Once I saw a herd of deer on a hillside.

The passengers chatted amongst themselves but my mother stayed silent, staring out over the water to the east shore. There were no other young people on the barge. I worked steadily through the first of the problems my class teacher had set for me: calculating the energy involved in moving the barge. I then walked carefully along the gunwale round the open hold, and sat in the bows and sang.

I like singing in the open air. I started with a sea shanty, which brought wry laughter from the bargees. The Loch was still and my voice echoed across the Glen. Then I sang a madrigal, taking each part in turn.

'Give us a real Song,' called one of the passengers when I'd finished.

I didn't like Singing in company if I wasn't with the choir. We're taught that Singing is a group activity; that to Sing on one's own is to draw attention to one's self. Worried, I looked at my mother. Go ahead, she said, nodding absently at me. I started to Sing my Stretch, softly at first but steadily building as I gained confidence. The gentle motion of the barge gave me the sense of a rising tide on a calm day, the water gently lapping over the exposed reefs. Without the rest of the choir, I had to find my own End Songs so I made the Stretch tail off to nothingness in both directions. The other passengers were quiet as I Sang, and smiled and clapped when I'd finished.

'You Sing well,' said one as I rejoined them. 'Just like your mother. Maybe you'll be picked as well.'

We ate at midday. The passengers had brought their own food but we all ate much the same things. Although the soil was fertile, we had a limited range of plants. Few animals and birds had survived the Event, and there were no fish in the Loch.

The afternoon passed slowly. There was little variation in the scenery. My father told us that the hills used to be covered in trees but they'd all been cut down to build great fleets of warships. Before the Event, tourists came to admire the barren scenery, not realising that they were visiting an unnatural disaster.

Rufus

It all seemed so simple.

We'd maybe three thousand people, with enough food and shelter, mostly. There was plenty of raw materials: mud; clay; stone; water; wood; fur; leather; wool; fat. But there was no consistent source of power other than trees and human muscle. So far, so Stone Age.

But unlike our Stone Age forebears, we also had frustrating quantities of arbitrary pre-Event artefacts. Useless solid state devices. Tantalising electric motors. Nary a steam engine. Far too few manual or clockwork machines. Lots of hand tools but never enough saws or drills.

And we had loads of scrap. Middens of wrecked cars and washing machines and fridges and televisions. Endless iron and wire and tyres and gear boxes and magnets. Buckets of screws and nuts and bolts and flanges. Plenty of glass but mostly broken. Everything was manky and needed to be painstakingly reclaimed.

So, what should be our priorities? More people of course. More people equals more muscle equals more social surplus. That's certainly simple: everyone enjoys fucking and we've no contraception.

Apart from more people, we desperately need electricity. With electricity we could haul our way back into the nineteenth century.

The obvious solution was to build a pumped water

generating plant. We could dam a burn to form a reservoir, and run the water down the hill through turbines into the Loch. When there was low demand for power we could use the excess to pump water back up the hill to keep the reservoir topped up.

No one thought this realistic: it would take far too many of us far too many years of back breaking work; a single scheme would never meet our demand for power so there'd be no prospect of keeping the reservoir topped up: we'd no big electric motors or pumps, and no way to manufacture them. But behind all these specious objections, I could see that nobody wanted to work any more than they did already.

I know I'm not good with people. Nobody ever seems to share my enthusiasms or my urgency. When faced with decisions, I come to quick, clear conclusions and am impatient at how long it takes others to agree with me. Often when I'm speaking, I can see people raising their eyebrows at each other, as if to say: 'He's off again.'

Andrew listened though. At first I thought it was because he wanted Grace. I didn't yet realise how much she wanted him.

It was Andrew who suggested building windmills, starting with a small one. I explained that lots of small windmills would be hopelessly inefficient. He said that one little windmill might just persuade people to build bigger ones.

Our first windmill was certainly modest. Barely two metres high, it housed the alternator from a lorry turned by a Savonius rotor made from the offset halves of an oil drum. We had wired the generator to a peculiar plastic lamp from a dusty collection in a sub-basement of what must have been the Town Hall.

Lots of people watched as the windmill took shape

but few offered to help. Sally was busy with Bonnie and Blythe. Typically, Grace kept aloof, despite her growing interest in Andrew.

The evening of the unveiling, a crowd of people stood and stared. We hadn't tested the rig beforehand, and knew the gentle mockery that awaited us if it failed. But we were younger and had o'erweening confidence in ourselves. As night fell, I threw the main switch and the ungainly lamp hummed into life. There was a shocked silence and then everybody laughed. The lamp was shaped like a woman with wings and a golden crown, holding a scroll bearing the message '*Adeste, Fideles*'.

People became excited, too excited, at all the things they might be able to do with even a limited power source. With a little persuasion, far less than I'd anticipated, we got broad agreement for a much longer term project I called The Bootstrapping. The idea was to build a large tower that could hold several windmills. Once the first windmill was running, we would use its output solely to drive electric tools to speed up the construction of the next one. Thus, as more mills came on stream, we would soon have spare power for other uses.

It was also agreed that Andrew and I would be fed by the community while we designed and constructed the large tower. When we needed more hands, we could call on others to help, and they would also be fed by the community in return.

I was so lost in new plans that I was taken aback when Andrew and Grace told me that they were setting up household together. And that Grace was pregnant. I had noticed that Andrew seemed increasingly distracted as we completed our small windmill, but I'd jollied him along. Perhaps I'd chivvied him along?

We decided to build the tower on the rise at the far end of The Fort. We were ready for a long, hard haul. I had estimated that it would take both of us working more or less non-stop the best part of three years to prepare the site, cut and dress enough wood, and build the first stage of the tower.

A strong sense of collectivity pervades our lives: we could not have survived so long without it. But that sense is usually only realised in extremes. Most of the time, people just seem to plod along as if mutual aid didn't exist. So when we started to clear and level the ground, I was astonished by how many people came to help. Something about the Bootstrapping connected with our zeitgeist. I only hope that one day we can recapture that connection.

We completed the first stage of the tower in under a year, and to a far higher standard than I'd expected. The timber gangs along the Loch sent us regular supplies of logs, which the Fort carpenters split and shaped. Increasingly, Andrew coordinated the ever changing construction team which assembled the platform, while I concentrated on designing the windmills it would house.

After that winter, everything changed. So much waste. So much death. Almost every household had been sundered. Sally and the girls survived, but Grace and Andrew gave up their daughter. Utterly bereft, Grace turned in on herself. Outwardly Andrew was stoical, but he began to visit the Arkists. We all know that Arkism is a syncretic fabrication, a harmless focus for that nagging need for answers that bedevils humans. But in the face of his grief, not even I had the heart to argue with him.

We persevered with the first windmill atop the platform, but its construction proved much harder than I had anticipated. Besides, we now mostly worked alone although nobody grudged us the resources to keep going.

Compared with our small windmill, we had

substantially increased the size of the rotor which now drove a bank of washing machine motors mounted on a common spindle. To my disappointment, the power output was far lower than I had predicted, and the wind variability meant that peak performance was rarely sustained.

Undaunted, I designed another windmill on top of a tall secondary tower, this time with large sails mounted on bearings to keep them facing the wind. The sails drove an automatic gear box to maintain constant torque as the wind speed changed. I should have spent longer designing the tower.

The new windmill rekindled my hopes. It gave steady power and could drive an electric drill. People once again became interested, and I started to plan the third windmill based on innovative changes to the second.

In retrospect, Andrew had been crazed by his daughter's death. As he spent more time with the Arkists, he became increasingly convinced of the imminent coming of the Great Flood. He cajoled me to help him build the new tower ever taller. He said it was to catch more of the wind but for all I knew it was to better scan the horizon for the white flecks of the scourging Waves.

Whenever the wind got up, Andrew would ascend the high tower. He claimed that the sails never stayed true for very long and that without regular trimming we would lose power. Lost in the next design, I paid little attention to him and realised too late that he had steadily extended the tower without broadening or strengthening it.

One afternoon, I was called urgently from the workshop and found Andrew lying in agony amongst the fragments of the high tower. A sudden gust of wind had toppled the structure, shattering Andrew's pelvis and all my dreams.

No blame accrued to me, not even from Grace. Andrew was characteristically staunch in his defence of the Bootstrapping. But it was made clear that I would enjoy no further community support.

It had all seemed so simple.

4 It was early evening when we reached the chain of locks at the far end of the Glen. I wanted to stay on the barge as it slowly descended down to the old sea level. It'll be quicker if we walk from here, said my mother. It took us the best part of an hour along the gravel tow path to my uncle's household on the far side of the Town. I was hungry and weary when we finally stopped.

Rufus and Sally had four daughters: Bonnie, Blythe, Goode and Gaye. Bonnie lived in a household near the Town basin where she worked as a tally clerk. Blythe was about to leave school when I last saw her. She was very grown up and had little time for her cousin from the country. Goode was a year younger than I and had been very anxious to make friends with me. She'd once said she hated having elder sisters and wished that Gaye had been a brother; Gaye dwelt in a dreamy world that Goode had long outgrown.

My mother knocked on the front door and Rufus opened it.

'You're early!' he said, hugging my mother.
'The wind blew fair,' said my mother, holding him close. 'It's so good to see you.'
'Come in, come in,' said Rufus, taking our bags.

We followed him through to the living room.

'Gaye! Goode!' called Rufus. 'They're here!'

The girls emerged from the rear of the cottage. Goode had grown taller and leaner. She stood to one side, smiling shyly at us. Gaye seemed little changed.

'Have you brought us a new story?' Gaye asked, tugging at my mother's leather bag.

'All in good time,' said her father.

'Have you eaten?'

'Not since lunch,' said my mother.

'Sit down, sit down,' said Rufus.

'I'll get the food,' said Goode.

I followed her through to the kitchen.

'How have you all been?' I asked, as she took a haunch of venison from the cold store.

'It's been a lot easier since Blythe left,' said Goode. 'I think she blames dad for mum's death. There was nothing he could do, of course.'

'Where's she gone to?' I asked.

'She's working in the Store,' said Goode. 'You'll probably see her the morn.'

'How's yourself?' I asked.

'Lonely,' she said. 'I miss mum. And dad's never really been the same. He's very protective of Gaye and mostly doesn't notice me. And you?'

She carved generous slices from the haunch.

'I'm lonely as well,' I said.

As she served out hefty portions of vegetables from a large casserole, I told her about my encounters with the Colonists, and how unsettled they left me. I didn't dwell unduly on the red-headed girl. Goode seemed intrigued by the noise from the radio.

'You should ask dad about it,' she said.

Supper was surprisingly lively. My mother was far more animated than I'd seen her since our flood. She and Rufus slipped back into what must have been a long familiar banter. I ate steadily and said little. Whenever I met Goode's eye she smiled at me. When we'd finished, my mother leant back in her chair.

'That was well worth the journey!' she said to Goode. 'Thank you!'

'The vegetables were all from Sally's field,' said Gaye. 'We spent ages choosing them.'

Goode got up and started to clear the table.

'What are your plans?' asked Rufus.

'I want to go to the Store,' said my mother, 'and start restocking my shelves.'

'Can you stay for the meeting?' said Rufus. 'I'd really like it if you could make it.'

'It depends on when the barge goes back,' said my mother. 'I'm in the middle of a new book and this one can't afford to skive any more school.'

'You could come to school with me,' said Goode.

'He'd miss the choir,' said my mother. 'It's not so long 'til the Autumn Singing.'

'Does he take after you?' asked Rufus. 'Might he be chosen?'

'I fear so,' said my mother. 'Not that his father would mind.'

'How's himself?' asked Rufus.

'Och, he's well enough,' said my mother, 'but he spends so much time at the new Ark. He's becoming more and more fatalistic and superstitious. I think he's lost any faith he ever had in the Project.'

'What's the Project?' I asked.

'Don't you tell him anything?' said Rufus.

'Not if I can help it,' said my mother. 'He'll find out when he's good and ready.'

'Find out what?' I asked, alarmed.

'Not now,' said my mother.

'Do you like how we live?' said Rufus to me, ignoring my mother.

'It's alright,' I said. 'We get by.'

'Don't you find it frustrating,' said Rufus, 'reading about how things used to be and how they could be? Don't you ever wonder about how things might be different?'

'Like the Colonists?' I said.

My mother snorted.

'At least they try,' said Rufus. 'No, not like the Colonists. Supposing the Event had never happened.'

'But it did happen,' I said.

'Well, supposing it could be reversed,' said Rufus.

'That's not possible,' I said.

'Why not?' said Rufus.

'We don't have enough people or energy,' I said.

'Are you sure?' said Rufus. 'Supposing we organised things differently.'

'But we've just enough people to grow all the food we need,' I said.

'We've got plenty of people,' said Rufus. We just don't use them well.'

'What do you mean, 'use them'?' I asked. 'People aren't things that one uses.'

'Are you so sure?' said Rufus.

'That's enough,' said my mother. 'Why don't you go and help your cousin?'

'Wash or dry?' asked Goode, back in the kitchen.

'Wash,' I said, stacking dishes into the sink. 'You know, the Colonists would build a machine to do this.'

'There are dishwashers in the Store,' said Goode, 'but they look like they'd need an awful lot of power.'

I filled the sink with hot water and started to wash up. I was puzzled by what Rufus had said and didn't understand why my mother was being so evasive.

'What's the Project' I asked finally.

'You won't believe me,' said Goode.

'Of course I'll believe you,' I said. 'Why shouldn't I?'

'Do you really like your life?' asked Goode. 'It didn't sound that way earlier.'

'What's the alternative?' I replied.

'To escape,' said Goode, bluntly.

'To escape?' I echoed, baffled. 'Why would we want to escape?'

'You heard dad,' said Goode. 'Its really dismal living this way, knowing how things could be.'

'But in two or three generations there'll be enough people to have another go at Bootstrapping,' I said. 'Then things should get much better.'

'But we won't be here to see it,' said Goode. 'Why shouldn't things be better for us as well?'

'Things aren't so bad,' said I. 'You know what it used to be like. Now we've always got enough to eat and we're mostly dry and warm. And we don't all have to work all the time just to get by.'

'Come on!' said Goode. 'Two hundred years ago my mum would still be alive and your father would still be walking. We've lost so much. Maybe it would be better if we didn't know how much.'

'So where could we escape to?' I asked.

'I don't know,' said Goode, 'But there must be something better than this.'

We finished cleaning up in silence and rejoined Rufus and my mother. Gaye had already gone to bed. Suddenly very tired, I sat down, stifling a yawn.

'You should get some sleep,' said Rufus. 'There are spare beds in Goode's and Gaye's rooms, but Gaye wakes up early and can be a bit noisy.'

'I'll go in with Gaye,' said my mother, turning to Goode. 'You don't mind sharing with him do you?'

'That's fine,' said Goode. 'I'll get off now though. I've some school work to finish.'

'Is she all right?' asked my mother, after Goode had left.

'She's not very happy,' said Rufus. 'She's far more intense than her big sisters ever were. I just don't know what to say to her.'

'Does she have many friends,' asked my mother.

'There's no one she's really close to,' said Rufus. 'I think she finds her school mates dull and self-absorbed. It's good that you're both here. She's especially pleased to see you,' looking at me.

I had increasing misgivings about our whole visit. No one had asked me where I wanted to sleep. I was fond of Goode, in so far as one can be fond of someone one sees briefly every couple of years. I had a vague feeling that something more was expected of me but I'd no idea what.

My uncle smiled at my confusion.

'Don't look so serious,' he said. 'Oh, I've got one for you. What's the difference between an anti-scorbutic and a long wait?'

'I've no idea,' I said.

'One's a tot of lime and the other's a lot of time,' said Rufus.

'That's awful,' I said. 'And I've got one for you.'

'Do tell,' said Rufus.

'What's the difference between a dead sheep and a load of fuel?'

'I've no idea,' said Rufus.

'One's a pile of meat and the other's a mile of peat,' said I.

Rufus and my mother groaned, animatedly.

'Much better,' said Rufus.

I stood up.

'I'll be off now,' I said.

'Sleep well,' said my mother. 'We've an early start.'

'It's very good to see you again,' said Rufus.

I unearthed my sleeping bag and went through to Goode's room. She was already in bed, her face to the wall. The other bed was made up. I blew out the candle and undressed quickly. In the books my mother read, people often wore special clothes in bed, which must cause a lot of extra washing and mending.

I slipped into bed and curled up. It was cold in the bed. I shut my eyes and silently Sang my Corner Song.

As my Song came full cycle, the Waves whispered from Corner to Corner, slow and regular as the last sighs of the Mid-Song Storm faded away. When my Song reached its beginning, I stretched out, ready to sleep.

'Are you still awake?' asked Goode, quietly.

'Just about,' I replied.

'I'm cold,' said Goode.

'I've warmed up a bit,' said I.

'Then I'll join you,' said Goode, slipping in beside me.

5 When my mother woke me next morning, Goode had gone. After a shower and a quick breakfast, we walked across Town to the Store with Rufus. Occasionally, people greeted us, but we didn't stop to talk with them.

The Town was very like our Village, if bigger and more orderly. The old Town had been flattened by the Event. As the ruins were cleared, stone and wooden houses had been built on the old plan of three parallel streets with connecting lanes between them. The largest building was the Ark; far more solid and imposing than my father's and even less likely to float.

The Store ran alongside the quay, on the site of the quay-side warehouses. It was stocked with gleanings from the old Town and organised on principles of utility. Many items were plentiful, especially building supplies, and simple plastic and metal objects. There was also considerable electric technology which could be stripped down for mechanical or structural components. All these were freely available to anyone that needed them. Less common items, like tools and ceramics, could be exchanged for produce. Typically a household or a community would pool food or handicrafts to acquire something for shared use. Access to very scarce items was controlled by the people that knew how to use them. Pre-electric machines were particularly prized. Most had been salvaged from the Town museum's basement: hand cranked calculators; foot operated dentist's drills; treadle sewing machines; mechanical typewriters; mincers; coffee grinders. My mother used a typewriter in the Fort.

Blythe met us outside the Store. Self assured, she barely noticed me.

'Hello!' she said to my mother. 'What are you after?'

'Reference books,' said my mother. 'Most of mine were lost or damaged in the flood.'

'What have you got for us?' said Blythe.

'I've a new children's story,' said my mother. 'And another three chapters of the novel.'

'What's the story like?' asked Blythe.

'Gaye enjoyed it,' said my mother.

'When did Gaye hear it?' I asked.

'This morning,' said my mother. 'While you were still in bed.'

'I was really tired,' I said.

'So was Goode,' said Rufus, pointedly.

'Have you made us copies?' asked Blythe, paying no attention to her father.

'I've got them here,' said my mother, patting the leather bag.

My mother and Blythe set off for the library. I stayed with Rufus. I knew my mother would brook no distractions.

'What would you like to do?' said Rufus.

'Don't you have to work?' I asked.

'I suppose I should,' said Rufus. 'but I don't often get to spend time with you and your mother.'

'She'll not be much company this morning,' I said.

'I can see that,' said Rufus. 'Why don't you come in with me. We can meet up with her later.'

Rufus worked in the warren of vaulted cellars under the Store. The cellars were weather proof and held our most precious resources.

As we walked across the yard, we passed a turner making bowls on a pedal-powered lathe. The blunt bit squeaked rhythmically as it rotated against the wood. Its cadence reminded me of my last afternoon on the moor. I began to whistle the sound from the

Colonists' radio.

Rufus stopped and turned to me.

'Where did you hear that?' he asked, surprised.

I quickly told him of my visits to the Colony.

'That's astonishing!' said Rufus. 'Come on!'

He led me down into an office lit from a skylight.

'You must listen to this!' he said, rummaging in a cupboard and handing me a plastic case. The cover read:

Power for the People! The Official Record of the Inauguration of the X-FLR6 High-Orbit Micro-wave Link.

The basements were served by an electric generator, powered by a huge tank of water. Anyone could use the electricity provided they replaced the water. It takes a lot of water to produce even a small amount of electricity. We did the sums at school.

Rufus went to the far side of the room, switched on a box bristling with wires and pulled on a long chain coming down from the ceiling. I could hear water starting to flow above us.

'Quick, bring it over here!' he said.

A small green light on the box began to glow. He took the case from me, opened it and took out a shiny disc which he fed into a slot on the front of the box. The box clicked and whirred. Suddenly I heard the sound from the moor, but this time it was answered by another, as if the two sounds were conversing. As the sounds faded, a voice began to speak:

For aeons, humanity has dreamt of boundless energy. Today, that dream is about to become a reality. . .

Rufus ejected the disc, shut down the water and turned off the box.

'Is that what you heard?' he asked me excitedly, putting the disc away.

'Well, the first part was the same,' I said, 'but I didn't hear the second bit.'

'Ah well,' said Rufus, plainly disappointed. 'I suppose we'd better go and pump some water.'

'What's wrong?' I asked him, as we went back out into the sunlight.

'There are records of people hearing the part you whistled,' said Rufus, 'but no one ever heard the second part. I was hoping that you'd heard it as well.'

'Why does it matter?' I asked.

'It might mean that we're not alone,' said Rufus. 'I don't suppose you can pedal with that leg.'

'No, I don't think so,' I said.

We stood beside the lower of two tanks. The generator's turbine sat in the fat plastic tube that connected them.

'It'll have to be the buckets then,' said Rufus, inspecting the meter on the side of the tube. 'We've used around forty.'

For the next hour, I filled buckets from the lower tank and Rufus winched them to the upper. We chatted while we worked. Rufus first asked me about my parents and how they were getting on. When I told him that they weren't, he laughed and said that he wasn't surprised. It had been hard being my mother's younger brother. My father had far more patience than he. In turn, I asked him about the Bootstrapping. He spoke animatedly about everybody's hopes for the high tower. He should have stopped my father climbing up to trim the sails as they swung into the wind.

When I mentioned the Project he became evasive so I asked him about the Colonists. He described the meeting when the Bootstrapping had been abandoned and how the minority had left to form their own community. When I described the adults who set my leg, he looked thoughtful. Both had been his friends and he regretted their parting. Neither of us mentioned Goode.

The time passed quickly. As we were finishing my mother joined us, a sack full of books slung over each shoulder.

'We better be off then,' she said to me, briskly.

'But I thought you were staying 'til the barge went,' said Rufus.

'It's leaving in half an hour,' said my mother. 'There's a special delivery for the Fort.'

Rufus looked at her oddly.

'You could always wait a few days for the next trip,' he said.

'We really need to get back now,' said my mother, firmly.

'Why are you in such a hurry?' said Rufus. 'The girls will be disappointed.'

'Och, they'll not notice,' said my mother.

Rufus turned to me.

'Would you like to stay yourself?' he said. 'You're very welcome.'

'He's got things to do,' said my mother, before I could answer. 'You should all come and visit us some time. It's really not so primitive.'

'We might just do that,' said Rufus.

'Why don't you go and get our bags,' said my mother to me, 'and we'll meet you back at the quay. There's a few things I need to discuss with Rufus.'

'About the Project?' I asked, in a futile act of self-assertion.

'Off you go,' said my mother.

I walked back to the house and let myself in. Gaye was sitting at the table, reading to herself. Goode was in the kitchen, leaning over the stove making soup. She looked up and smiled at me.

'You're back early,' she said.
'I'm afraid we're leaving,' I said awkwardly.

'My mother says she needs to get going.'

Goode stopped cooking.

'Why don't you stay yourself?' she said. 'Dad would be delighted. So would I.'
'I can't,' I said. 'Really, I can't.'
'Don't you want to stay?' said Goode. 'Was it last night?'

What could I say. That I didn't know what the previous night implied? That I was worried about my parents? That I wanted to go back to the Colony? That above all I needed to Sing?

I walked across to her and held her close. She clung to me, then gently pushed me away. At arms length, she looked me in the eye, nodded sadly and turned back to the stove.

I picked up the bags and left. I didn't know where we'd meet again or what we'd have to say to each other. I felt that everything had changed. I didn't understand why. I still don't.

Down at the quay, my mother and I said perfunctory goodbyes to Rufus and boarded the barge. We seemed to be the only passengers. The deck was empty apart from a large wooden box.

The wind had changed since the previous day. I watched the Town grow smaller as the barge made its way along the coast towards the locks. Once we were inside each lock, the bargees closed the gates behind us and opened the sluice in front. Lock by lock, the barge slowly rose to the level of the Loch.

My mother sat and read under the canopy. Alone in the bows I tried to Sing. My voice was strong and clear but I was apart from the Song, my mind reeling with the last several hours.

Half way along the Loch the wind died. The bargees cursed and broke out the oars. Soft from weeks of rest, my hands chafed and blistered as I pulled in time to the barge master's chant.

6 It was long dark when we reached the Village basin. The bargees helped us ashore. As they passed us up our bags, I heard the barge master tell my mother,

'Don't worry. We'll make sure you get them.'

We walked home in silence. As we neared our house, my mother suddenly stopped.

'I know you've lots of questions,' she said to me.

I looked at her helplessly.

'Why won't you trust me?' I asked.

'Of course I trust you,' she said, 'You have to trust me. Things will become clearer after the Singing, I promise you.'

'Why did you take me with you?' I asked.

'Why do you think?' she asked in return.

'You clearly didn't need my company,' I said.

She watched me patiently.

'Why did we go there so suddenly?' I asked. 'And why did we leave so quickly?'

'You could have stayed,' she said.

'Could I?' I asked.

'Of course!' she said. 'Why didn't you say you wanted to?'

'You didn't give me much choice,' I said.

She studied me carefully.

'Did you want to stay?' she asked.

I hesitated.

'No,' I said, finally.

'Right,' she said. 'So let's go in.'

When I hadn't been Singing on the barge, I'd listened to the Loch breathing. Its long, undulating shoreline has a gentle, rhythmic Song, broken where the streams and rivers come off the mountains.

After the next choir practice, I talked with our choir teacher about how the shape of the Loch formed its Song. He said that I should now be able to feel the shape of my own Stretch when I Sang it. I asked if I could borrow the map of my Stretch. He suggested that, instead, I should look for my Stretch on the shores beyond the Gate.

Back at home, I announced that I wasn't going to school the next day. My siblings twittered at me, eager to know what I planned. When I told them, my father said that beyond the Gate there was nothing but a vast, sterile, expanse of grey baked mud. When the Great Flood came, the Ark would carry us all across it. Until then we were all far safer at home. My mother smiled grimly. Let him be, she said. He knows what he's got to do.

The next morning, I was surprised to find that my mother hadn't yet gone to work. After breakfast, we walked together to the Fort, taking it in turns to push the bicycle. At the base of the Fort, she rested the bicycle against the cliff.

'Before you go,' said my mother, 'I need to explain something to you. I Sang well when I was your age. Like you, I went in search of my Stretch but I couldn't find it. I began to suspect that I'd never truly feel the Song inside me and that I was far better off with words. I've watched you Singing and I've seen how, more and more, your Song becomes you. Words come alive in my brain the way the Song does in yours. That's why I wouldn't join the Wave Singers. Maybe you have the temperament. Maybe. But it's a hard calling and there's no way back from it. Is that what you really want?'

'I've no idea what I want,' I said bluntly.

My mother looked at me quietly. Then she passed me a backpack from the bicycle pannier.

'I brought you some lunch,' she said. 'You better be off.'

She embraced me and started up the steps. I hefted the pack and set off along the edge of the South Dyke away from the Fort, past the midden to the Gate. I'd often looked out down the Firth from the top of the South Dyke but had never ventured beyond the Gate. At the Gate, radial paths separated the triangular fields. I took the central track that led straight across the plain. The land was noticeably poorer than ours. The fields were smaller and the crops were thinner. When the Loch was high, irrigation pipes brought water past the Gate but during the dry season the farmers had to rely on their meagre rainwater reservoirs.

As I walked, I thought about my father. I'd been very small when he fell from the high tower and I could only remember him stoical in his wheelchair. He sought comfort in our family and solace in the Ark, but he still ached for the wind in the sails. On clear winter days, he'd sit outside and watch the breeze catch the smoke from the chimneys.

After a while I reached the rough stone wall that marked the edge of the fields. I crossed the stile at the end of the path and stepped out onto the un-tilled bed of the Firth. Our choir teacher had told me to keep walking, following the line of the path, until I was equidistant between the ends of my Stretch. I asked him how I'd recognise the ends. He said I'd know them when I saw them.

Our teacher seemed to hint at some experience that would

transform my understanding of my Stretch. His air of mystery seemed ridiculous. With the sea long gone and the shore eroded, all I could hope to find was the barest suggestion of my Stretch's former bounds.

As I walked, I thought about my mother. She rarely spoke of her calling as a Wave Singer but I was sure it ran deep inside her. At the Spring Singings she was quickly lost in the rhyme of the windlass. I wondered what she'd really found when she went looking for her Stretch.

I knew from the map that a river once ran down the centre of my Stretch and that a small Town had stood at its mouth. At school, they told us that many of the townspeople had worked in a factory that processed chemicals from the big cities beyond the mountains. The chemicals were held in large concrete tanks. The Event shattered the tanks and strewed the chemicals across the sundered landscape. Since then, nothing had grown on the lands beyond the Fort.

As I walked, I thought about what my uncle had said about not using people well. Had Goode used me well? She could have chosen anyone in the Town. Why had she chosen me?

The Firth steadily widened and the sea bed sloped gently away from me. I followed it downwards, all the time watching the shape of the coastline to my right. My Stretch included the Head and the Bar. I knew from the map that both had been narrow tongues of land curving out from the shore and then running parallel to it, bounding deep stony inlets that drained the coastal marshes. Water would flow quickly into the inlets with the rising tide's backwash and out slowly as the tide fell.

As I walked, I thought about the girl with the red hair and the large feet. She seemed utterly disinterested in anything beyond the Colony's search for a way to transcend the Event. She certainly seemed utterly disinterested in me.

The sun was high and my leg felt weary. I sat down cross-legged and opened the bag my mother had packed for me. The bag held a bottle of water and a cabbage tortilla. I took a long pull at the water and looked around. I could still see the Fort and the Gate in the distance behind me. Beyond both shores, the mountains rose up from the narrow plains. At school they told us that, after the battle on the moor, the people were driven from the mountains, fled down the Firth and crossed the oceans on boats built from the trees they'd felled.

On the way out from the Gate, the coast had seemed smooth and featureless. Now, as I lazily surveyed the shoreline, I noticed a subtle change directly opposite me. The land seemed to dip down and up again, like the crease in a blanket left by a fold. I scanned the shoreline from side to side. To my right, back towards the Fort, I spotted a faint fracture line along the sand dunes. I looked to my left and found a similar line, the same distance away from the dip in the shoreline. If the fold was once the river, and the lines were once the spits, then perhaps this was my Stretch. I stood up and began to Sing.

At the end of my Stretch, I felt tired and disappointed. I'd hoped that finding the lineaments of my Stretch would make it whole inside me. I knew I'd Sung well yet I knew my Singing was still lifeless, like one of the Colonist's machines. Perhaps this was what my mother had felt when she went looking for her Stretch. How could the Song ever hope to recapture the shore-girth sea? Perhaps the Song was never more than an empty nostalgia for a past that never had been. I sat down and ate the tortilla. When I'd finished eating, I drained the bottle and turned back towards the Village.

As I walked, I thought about myself. I had never really

questioned the constraints of our circumstances. I had always accepted the way things were, the way we made slow but steady progress from a fearful past. Now I no longer knew where that progress led. Until this day I'd thought I could be a Wave Singer and that the Song bore meaning. Now everything seemed grey and hard and flat, like the long-dead bed of the Firth.

My leg ached badly as I crossed the stile and followed the path to the Gate. Through the Gate and round the South Dyke, I saw my mother sitting at the foot of the steps that led up to the Fort.

'Did you find it?' she asked, standing up and joining me.

'I think so,' I said.

'Aren't you sure?' she asked, taking the bag from me and putting it back into the bicycle pannier.

'Well, it looked right,' I said.

'Did you Sing?' she asked, righting the bicycle.

'Of course I Sang,' I said, taking hold of the handlebars.

'So what happened?' she asked, as we set off.

'I just Sang,' I said, flatly. 'What was supposed to happen?'

My mother looked relieved. Then she looked sad.

'When I found my Stretch. . .' she began.

'But you said you didn't find it!' I said, outraged.

'When I found my Stretch,' she continued, 'when I Sang, nothing else mattered. The world dissolved and my Stretch filled me.'

'Why did you tell me you didn't find it?' I said, very angry. 'Why did you lie to me?'

'Why do you think?' she replied calmly.

Speechless with rage, I dropped the bicycle and fled from her.

Grace

I loathe this existence. I fear I'll never cease to
grieve; I know I'll never lightly leave. Why am I
grieving? For my first born. Why can't I leave?
Because I'm here.

My first born was a beautiful baby girl. We'd so badly
wanted a girl. And when I felt her wriggling and
giggling inside me, I knew she was a girl with the smug
irrational certainty that I utterly despise in others.

Andrew says we made the only possible decision;
he says we have other beautiful children. Of course
he's right.

The winter she was born was unspeakably harsh.
Everything froze. The days were clear and bright
but the ground never thawed. We told ourselves
we'd have enough fuel and food; we'd seen hard
winters before but they'd never lasted long.

The fuel began to run low, so we stopped heating
the barns. Then the animals began to sicken. To
stop the disease spreading, we killed and burned
the sick animals. And we fed up the remainder to
try to keep them healthy. When we started to run
out of feed, we slaughtered and ate the healthy
animals one by one, until we had only a few dozen
breeding pairs left.

Next people began to fall ill. First the elderly. Surely
one might live more than fifty years. They knew what
we all faced. After all, they had told us the harrowing
tales of their parents' childhoods; in those not so far
off days, people had been rather less squeamish in the
teeth of starvation. So now they said we should lay

them out in the sun, that they might see it set and hope to see it rise once more. We argued with them. We pled with them. And we helped them out beyond The Gates, and wrapped them up warmly, and left them facing West.

The sickness slowly spread. I was still weak from the birth, my breasts dried up, and my beautiful baby girl couldn't keep down our precious ewe's milk. Stone faced, I held her in my arms as she screamed with hunger. Andrew wept as he gently carried her out to join her grandparents.

I didn't want to have any more children but I knew I had to. Nobody forced me. It was my duty.

We yearned so much for another girl. Another girl would be a fresh start. And girls can bear more girls: all boys can do is pump and squirt, not that pumping entirely lacks merit.

This time I tried not to think about whether the wriggling giggler was a boy or a girl. As Andrew said, every child was wanted and we could always try again. But when they proffered me my beautiful baby boy I felt nothing more than broken resignation and deep shame at my disappointment. But I picked up the pieces. What else could I do?

More pumping begat more bairns. First the girl, by now her birth more a relief than a delight. At least there'd be someone to carry on the household. Why did that matter so much?

After the girl came the twins, another boy and girl: there have always been twins in both our lines. Four children filled the house. And for a while everything seemed so hopeful. Of course it was all forlorn.

We'd gambled everything on the Bootstrapping. We all thought there was no other way forward, Andrew more than most. Look at him now, marooned in his wheelchair. Oh, he was a lovely man, tall and strong, brown and wiry, high in the breeze atop the tallest tower. After I lost my beautiful girl, I couldn't have gone on without him and now he shan't go on without me.

Of course I love the boy. He is my eldest child. How could I not love him?

He's certainly bright and willing. He's a hard worker. He always does what's asked of him. He's polite and thoughtful and generous.

But the boy worries me. He seems to have no friends, nobody he wants to spend time with. He rubs along well enough with other people, but he barely engages with them and he never initiates anything. Sometimes his passivity enrages me, and I become cold and rational. Then I hate myself.

Andrew says I should let him be, that he's not driven like me and Rufus. Yet Andrew thinks he's the makings of a Wave Singer: Andrew has no idea how driven Wave Singers are.

Since he came back from the Colony the boy seems changed. Now he asks lots of questions. Why do we do things this way? Why don't we do things differently? Why do we choose this way to live? Why don't we live like the Colonists?

Of course questions are good! And these are good questions. But they feel sharp and accusatory, as if we haven't explained anything to him, or offered him any choices at all. Yes, our explanations and options are self-serving. We've survived this way and, above all, we want our children to survive.

What sort of life is this? We survive, but to what end? We know all the things we've lost. We know that neither our children nor their children will live any differently. And we know that their lives will be blighted by that self-same crippling knowledge. But we cannot in good conscience leave them in ignorance.

Perhaps I should have left when that sad Spring

finally came, after we went out beyond The Gates, and buried our past and future. There was nowhere else to go. I like solitude but I have never been solitary: I have too strong a sense of my own life intertwined in everybody else's.

So in my grief I withdrew into words. Other peoples' words that told of worlds that might have been and might be. Other people's words that came alive for me and helped my own words come alive for other people. Slowly I gathered up all the books I could find. I read every last one and shelved them and catalogued them.

Books are no different from anything else we hold in common. Anyone can always come and take them away. And books are dead unless they're read. But more and more they became my books, in my mind as well as in other peoples'. Now my empty shelves cry out to be filled.

There are lots of books in the Town. Every time they open another cellar they find more, squirreled away. Nobody begrudges me them, provided I make them new stories in return.

I should go to the Town. Rufus's last letter felt morose, his jaunty bluffness forced. I'll find out when the barge next leaves.

Andrew won't come. I won't even bother to ask him. He won't say anything against Rufus but he can't abide mention of Rufus's schemes, saying false hope is worse than none.

Certainly, no one can accuse the Arkists of false hope; I really can't thole their fortitude, certain of a doom they can't deflect, embracing ritual they know to be pointless. But stuck in his chair, trying to hold the household together, perhaps the Ark is Andrew's best solace. If only he could read their Book as a fable, as an allegory.

Of course I blame myself.

7 I saw little of my mother before the market. She spent most of her time in the Fort, typing up copies of her new story.

My mother still hadn't read the story to us. I want it to be a surprise, she said. You can hear it at the market, like everyone else.

The market was held in the Parade Ground, below the stone-clad earthworks. Every household had their own wooden booth. On market day, they un-shuttered the windows and displayed their wares. Then everybody walked round all the booths, eyeing up how much had been produced and deciding what they particularly wanted. There was always demand for our vegetables. We always needed candles, soap and salt.

People took orders at the market for things it took longer to make. Last time, I had ordered a new pair of shoes. The best shoes were soled with car tyres; the old Town's midden was full of them.

We pushed my father to the market, boxes of vegetables stacked on his knees. Our booth was painted green: deep and dark at the base shading to a pale turquoise at the crown of the roof. We took down the shutter and fixed it horizontally in front of the open window. Then we laid out our vegetables on the shutter, stacking the empty crates inside the booth.

I offered to take my father round to look at the other booths. Much time was always spent at the market tallying what was on offer and reckoning what would be fair exchanges. Everybody knew what everything was worth because everybody knew how long it took to make things. It was understood that nobody would produce anything that other people wouldn't want. By the end of the market, nobody would be left with anything they'd brought with them.

My father said he wanted to stay at our booth. He asked us to fetch him when my mother was ready to read her new story.

I walked slowly round the market. The other booths were decorated according to the whims of their occupants. One was blue and fluted like a police box. Another was clad entirely in fragments of mirror. A third was woven from withy branches. I made my way towards the Colonist's booth on the opposite side of the Parade Ground. Their booth was sleek and functional. The shutter, balanced by weights, articulated on iron hinges. The Colonists rarely came to the market but that day their shutter was open.

As I crossed the Parade Ground, I saw my mother mounting the wooden stage. We had said little to each other since my venture beyond the Gate. I walked quickly back to our booth and trundled my father across the sandstone flags. My mother had already sat down and opened her leather bag. Everybody left the booths and crowded round the stage. My mother began to read:

The Buddha and the Robot

Long ago when the world was old, the Buddha sat under a mushroom. One day, the robot came across the plain.

'Hello Buddha,' said the robot. 'Hello Robot,' said the Buddha. 'I'm getting a bit fed up,' said the robot. 'What's the problem?' asked the Buddha. 'It's those elephants,' said the robot. 'They keep knocking me over. I wish I was a bit bigger. 'All right!' said the Buddha. And the robot began to grow.

Long ago when the world was old, the Buddha sat under a mushroom. One day, the elephants came across the plain. 'Hello Buddha,' said the biggest elephant. 'Hello elephants,' said the Buddha. 'We're

getting a bit fed up,' said the medium sized
elephant.' 'What's the problem?' asked the Buddha.
'It's that robot,' said the smallest elephant. 'It keeps
knocking us over. We wish we were a bit bigger.'
'Goodness me!' said the Buddha. 'You better go
and talk with Ganesh.'

The elephants travelled through the fabulous lands
to the court of Ganesh.

Long ago when the world was old, Ganesh sat on
his throne. 'Hello Ganesh,' said the biggest
elephant. 'Hello elephants,' said Ganesh. 'We're
getting a bit fed up,' said the medium-sized
elephant.' 'What's the problem?' asked Ganesh. 'It's
that robot,' said the smallest elephant. 'It keeps
knocking us over. We wish we were a bit bigger.'
'All right!' said Ganesh. And the elephants grew. . .

At that moment, there was a commotion behind us and two of
our neighbours propelled a strange bald woman through the crowd.
She was thin and elderly, dressed in a crude coat of the skins of
small furry animals. As the stranger drew close I saw that she had a
large 'T' branded on her forehead.

I had seen a branding when I was very young. A man had raped
a girl from the next Village. After we judged him, he was stripped
naked and held down. The iron brand glowed red in the fire. The
man screamed as the brand burnt into his flesh. Then he was carried
to the high rampart at the back of the Fort and forced over the
rusty barbed wire fence into the dead land beyond.

The strange woman was helped up onto the stage.

'Why were you branded?' asked our neighbour.
'I stole food,' said the woman.
'Why did you steal food?' asked our other neighbour.
'I was hungry,' said the woman.

'Was everybody else hungry?' asked my mother.

'Yes,' said the woman. 'Everybody else was hungry as well.'

'Why have you come back?' asked our neighbour.

The woman undid her coat. Her body was emaciated and her skin was covered in red, crusted, weeping sores.

'This is where I started,' said the woman. 'This is where I want to end.'

'There's nothing for you here,' said our other neighbour. 'You know that.'

'I know,' said the woman. 'I know.'

'Tell us where you've been,' said my mother.

'After I was branded,' said the woman, 'I headed south, following the line of the old road through the mountains. They're all bare. Nothing grows on them and there are no animals or birds. In the lower glens there's heather scrub. I was starving and grubbed for roots to fill my belly. Beyond the mountains there's thick bush. It was slow going but there was more to eat. Finally I reached the remains of a city on the shores of a dry Firth like ours. It was completely overgrown. I cleared some land in what must have been a park and I built myself a hut. I've lived there ever since.'

'Have you ever seen anybody else?' asked my mother.

'No,' said the woman. 'Nobody.'

'When did you get sick?' asked my mother.

'Late every summer, just before the rains, there's a hot wind from the north west,' said the woman. 'Usually it carries a light sandy dust. The mountains must shield us from it here. Two summers ago, the wind was much stronger and the dust was much darker and heavier. All the vegetation withered and died, and I started finding dead and dying rabbits outside the warren where I used to trap them. Then my gums started to bleed and my hair all fell out.'

'Radiation sickness,' said our neighbour.

'You know we can't help you,' said our other neighbour. 'No one can.'

'I've lived alone for too long,' said the woman. 'I don't want to die alone.'

'You can spend the night in the hut by the midden,' said my mother. 'We'll decide what's to be done in the morning.'

Nobody argued with my mother. What the woman had done was unpardonable but life was easier now.

'Won't you finish the story?' said my father.

'Not today,' said my mother, taking the handles of his wheelchair.

After our trip to the Town, my mother and father had slipped back into a companionable ease with each other. The white Arkles were never mentioned.

I left my parents and went round the stage to the Colonist's booth. The red-headed girl with the large feet was sitting beside a crate of rice spirits, reading. As I approached her, I whistled the noise from the radio on the moor. She looked up and whistled it back to me. I then whistled the response I'd heard with my uncle. She stood up and came across to meet me.

'Where did you hear that?' she exclaimed

I told her of my visit to the Town.

'Whistle it again,' she said.

I whistled the response. She took my arm.

'Come on,' she said. We need to go somewhere quiet.'

We left the Fort and followed the boardwalk to our Village. The Village was still; everybody was at the market. We walked across the paddies and out into the maize field that borders the Village land.

She sat down and removed her shoes.

'Take your shoes off and sit opposite me,' she said.

I did so. Then she leant forward and took my hands. Stretching out her feet until the heels pressed against mine, she looked me straight in the eyes and whistled the first sequence. I whistled the response. She whistled it back to me. I whistled it again. We whistled it together.

'That's it,' I said.
'Thank you,' she said.

Then she drew me across to her.

Later, she lay back and watched me dress.

'Will we see each other again?' I asked.
'That seems likely,' she said.
'Don't you want to see me again?' I asked anxiously.
'I don't mind,' she said.
'Do you think you could find out more about the sound we heard?'
'Does it really matter?' I asked, petulantly.
'Of course it matters!' she said.
'Why does it matter?' I persisted.
'The sound our radio picks up must be a signal from the satellite telling us that it's ready for further instructions,' she said. 'Maybe we could communicate with it.'
'What would be the point?' I asked in frustration. 'We wouldn't know how to instruct it even if we could talk to it.'
'That's why we need to find out more about how the signals work,' she said.
'But you've no way to generate the sounds,' I said. 'You'll need a computer for that.'
'There are computers in the Store,' she said.

'How are you going to power a computer?' I asked. 'Your sheep can't possibly keep walking for long enough.'

'You can whistle the response,' she said. 'Maybe we could wire up a microphone for you?'

'But don't I matter?' I asked.

'Don't be so silly!' she said. 'Could you pass me my plaid?'

8 I spent the summer days in the paddy fields and the evenings moping at home. I didn't know what to do with myself. I was tired of life in the Village but I couldn't live in the Town, trading one domesticity for another. And yet I couldn't live in the Colony, exchanging one isolation for another.

I was surly with my siblings and peevish with my parents. I felt increasingly dislocated from the Song and stopped going to choir practice. I began to read the novels my mother had brought back from the Town. They were a strange mix of historical romances, cowboy stories and detective fiction. I worked my way steadily through them. The plots and characters seemed the same: honour, virtue, wealth, status, pride and reputation; all were lost and found.

In the books my mother read, people thought too much about themselves. I always wanted to know what happened next.

Towards the end of the rice harvest, our choir teacher came to see me. He told me that our Village Song needed my Stretch. I said that they should find someone else to Sing it. He told me that I was being selfish and that there wasn't enough time for anyone else to learn my Stretch. Grudgingly, I said that I would stay in the choir until the Autumn Singing.

The next evening, after work, I went back to the choir. Everyone greeted me warmly, as if I'd been away on a long journey. The choir had improved considerably. My Singing had deteriorated markedly.

After the practice, I stayed behind and our choir teacher played me the steel recording of our Song. He told me that my Stretch was bound by all the other Stretches, as I was bound by the people around me. Every Stretch was linked equally to every other Stretch, and as each Stretch changed so did all the others, in sympathy or in dissonance. I accused him of sophism. People were far more than passive Stretches. Everybody made their own fate. He laughed and told me that everyone's fate flowed from the tensions with everyone else, not from individual choices. He also said that, originally, 'sophos' meant 'wise'.

As I walked home, I wondered if we were both right. If every Stretch influenced every other Stretch then perhaps I could shape our Song with my own Singing. I started to Sing as I worked in the paddy fields. As I Sang, I thought about my Stretch as part of the whole Song, and began to wonder how I could mould the whole Song through changes to my Stretch.

At choir practice, as I regained my confidence in my Singing, I began to introduce slight variations into the usual patterns of my Stretch, exaggerating the wash from the Head and the Bar, and the flow of the river that ran between them. The other Singers were puzzled. They had always been happy to repeat familiar phrases but now they began to adjust their Stretches, to pull mine back towards theirs. Our choir teacher was pleased. He said that our Village Song was finding new life and that the other choirs would be caught unaware.

The Autumn Singing was held in the Grand Magazine in the Fort. All the Villages of the Firth sent their choirs. The Singing was highly competitive and villagers were fiercely partisan.

On the stage in the Grand Magazine, each choir stood next to those that Sang the neighbouring Stretches. At the start of the Singing, all the choirs together sang the Firth. Then each choir sang their Village Song. After each Song, the audience cast votes for each choir except their own. Our choir always Sang last. Some people said that Singing last was best because the audience was getting tired and wouldn't notice mistakes. Others said that Singing last was worst because the audience was getting tired and wouldn't forgive mistakes.

At the end of each Autumn Singing, the oldest Wave Singer chose their successor from amongst the Singers. The person who was chosen would spend the next year Singing with the oldest Wave Singer. Just before the following Autumn Singing, the oldest Wave Singer would go back to their Village.

My father told us that being chosen as a Wave Singer was the highest honour. He said that Wave Singing was our only thread back to the past and that the Wave Singers told us who we are. We already know who we are, said my mother, running her fingers up and down the soft brown hair on the nape of his neck.

On the afternoon of the Autumn Singing, I left the paddy fields much earlier than usual and joined the choir for a last practice. We then walked to the Fort and took our place on the stage, to the right at the front.

The Grand Magazine was full. The Wave Singers sat along the front row of the raked wooden benches. The Villagers of the Firth filled the rest of the seats. At the last Autumn Singing, the Village across the Firth from us had won. This year, many people from our Village had come to cheer us on. I could see my father and siblings waving at me. I'll try to come, said my mother, but I'll need to meet the barge first.

I felt at ease on the stage. I knew that I was a skilful but unexceptional Singer, and that I was unlikely to be chosen. I had decided to stop Singing and to ask if I could work on the barge.

As always, we started the Firth calm and still. Then we steadily built a surging tide and a strengthening gusty wind. As the Singing intensified, our choir began to nudge our Song away from the neighbouring Songs. The other choirs were nervous and started to make mistakes as they tried to follow us. At the end of the Firth, most of the audience was restless but the Wave Singers in the front row were looking animatedly at our choir.

We sat patiently while the other choirs Sang in turn. All of the other choirs Sang well. One Singer, from the branded woman's Village, had a particularly strong, clear voice which carried their Song. I was sure that she would be chosen by the oldest Wave Singer.

When it was our turn to Sing, we stood up and formed our Strand. The two End Singers began their Stretches, and the rest of the choir joined them, in sequence along the Strand. I was in the centre of the Strand, and took up my own Stretch, intertwining it with the Stretches on either side of me.

As our Song gained momentum, I shut my eyes in concentration, and had the sudden sensation of looking down, above the Fort, above the Village, above the Firth, above the Island, above the oceans, above the continents, above the small bluey-green ball circling the yellow sun, above the sea of stars, above endless black space.

As I Sang, my Song filled the void, a galaxy formed from the nothingness, a bright star burst into being on the outer rim of the galaxy and nine planets coalesced around the shrinking star. As I Sang, great land masses twisted across the oceans on the third planet and the continents collided, thrusting up mountains where the terranes of our Island ground together. As I Sang, new continents twisted away from each other, forming great volcanic vents on the ocean edge of our Island. As I Sang, the seas rose and fell, and the glaciers swallowed and spat out our Island, carving out our Glen.

As I Sang, the first people came over the mountains, following the sheep and deer. As I Sang, brochs became castles and clachans, and black houses became mansions and tower blocks. As I Sang, the Great Flood levelled our Island, the Last People came down from the mountains and began all over again.

I suddenly became aware that nobody else was Singing; I stopped and opened my eyes. Everyone in the Grand Magazine was watching me. One of the Wave Singers stood up and walked forward to the foot of the stage.

'You'll do,' she said.

I looked across the audience to my family. My siblings were chattering excitedly. My father was beaming, tears rolling down his face. My mother was sombre. Next to her sat Rufus and Goode. Goode was cradling her bairn-bumped belly. She smiled up at me.

'Shall we go?' said the Wave Singer.

Drained and trembling, I left the stage and followed her along the central aisle, through the raked seats and out round the Barrack Rooms into the central Barrack Square.

'Let's sit down,' said the Wave Singer.

I joined her on the wrought iron bench. It was a still clear night. The Milky Way traversed the sky.

'What happened to me in there?' I asked.

'It looked like you found your Stretch,' said the oldest Wave Singer.

'Where were you when you were Singing?'

'Everywhere and nowhere,' I told her.

'How did it feel?' she asked me.

'Overwhelmingly vast and empty,' I said.

'How did it feel?' she asked again.

'Strangely familiar,' I said, 'and utterly alien.'

'How did it feel?' she asked for a third time.

'I was just there,' I said. 'You must know.'

'I was there once,' she said sadly, 'but that was a long time ago now.'

'Haven't you been there since?' I asked, taken aback.

'No,' she said. 'Never. None of us ever has, even though we spend the rest of our lives trying.'

'But you must be able to!' I said, distraught. 'Why can't you?'

'I don't know,' she said. 'Sometimes I think it's because we try too hard. It becomes an obsession, an addiction. My Wave Singer tried to warn me. I wouldn't listen to him. I hope you'll listen to me. Watch now.'

She took a small brass disk out of her waistcoat pocket and placed it flat on the palm of her left hand. Then she sang a pure, rising note that disappeared beyond my hearing. The brass disk rose up from her palm. She drew breath, and the disk dropped back.

'What did you see?' she asked.

'The disk rose,' she said.

'Did the disk rise or did you see the disk rise?' she asked.

'I don't understand,' I said.

'Did you find your Stretch or did you Sing in the Hall?' she asked.

'You're trying to confuse me,' I said.

'No,' she said. 'It's very simple. You saw the disk rise and I saw you Sing in the Hall. But no one except you saw your Stretch. I can teach you how to make the disk rise but I can't teach you how to find your Stretch.'

She sang at the disk again. I reached out and plucked the disk from the air. It was a £50 coin from before the Event. There were cases of them in the Store.

'So what should I do?' I asked.

'If you come with me,' she said, 'I'll tell you everything I know. You don't have to decide now. But if you don't join me before the next Autumn Singing, I'll choose someone else. What do you want to do?'

'I want to find my Stretch again,' I said.

'All Wave Singers ever want to do is to find their Stretch,' said the oldest Wave Singer. 'That's why they're no good for anything else.'

'They're good at making Arkles,' I said, thinking of my father.

'Exactly,' she said. 'Anyway, it's time for the prize giving. Are you coming?'

'I think I'll stay out here a bit longer,' I said.

'You know where to find me,' she said.

She got up and went back across the Barrack Square.

9 I sat alone beneath the baleful stars. I couldn't bear my father's fulsome praise or my mother's silent scorn. I couldn't thole my uncle's hopeless cheer or my cousin's desperate love. And I couldn't face the Wave Song's endless lure.

Perhaps the Colonists were right and all we could do was to guddle for the dawn in the dusk. But there might still be some means of escape if we didn't just accept things as they were. Maybe I could find out how to talk to the satellite. Maybe then the girl with the red hair and the large feet would have more time for me.

When I heard the audience starting to leave the Grand Magazine, I got up and crossed the square to the steps down to the boardwalk. At the foot of the steps, I turned towards the Gate.

There was a light in the window of the midden hut. Ever since she'd interrupted my mother's story, the woman with the brand on her forehead had lived there. No one had asked her to leave. She spent her days sorting through the mounds of rubbish. Every so often, someone from her former household brought her supplies.

Once a week, my father visited the woman in the midden hut. One of us would push him along the boardwalk but we were never invited in. Whenever we asked him what they talked about, he was unusually silent. What's it to you, said my mother, grating her finger nails across his stubbly chin.

I walked over to the hut and knocked on the door.

'Who's there?' she called.
'Can I come in?' I said.

'No one's stopping you,' she said. 'The door's open.'

I let myself in and looked around. The woman was sitting on the bed. The hut was very small. The bed was a mattress made from discarded rice sacks stuffed with maize chaff.

'Have a seat,' she said, gesturing towards a misshapen metal frame woven with knotted lengths of frayed electric cable. 'I don't often have visitors. What brings you here?'

'I wanted to ask you about the city you lived in,' I said, sitting down.

'Ask away,' she said.

'Did you ever come across anything that might have been a communications centre?' I said, cautiously.

'There's a big hill in the centre of the city,' said the woman, 'with what looks like the remains of concrete buildings and a tumbled down tower. I never found anything useful up there. The views are good though.'

'How long would it take to get there?' I asked.

'About a week if the weather holds,' said the woman, 'but you don't want to go there.'

'I need to go there,' I said. 'I can't stay here any longer.'

'You're crazy!' said the woman. 'Whatever you've done, you're far better off staying here if you can, believe me!'

'I haven't done anything,' I said. 'That's the sum of it. But I need to do something now.'

'If you must go,' she said, 'you should leave well before the snows or you won't get back through the mountains. Follow the road until you come to a wide river bed, then follow the coast towards the sea. The Firth narrows and widens again. You'll find my patch just before you get to the stumps of the first bridge. Take enough food and water for the journey. Once you get there, there should still be enough to eat and the rain should have washed away all the dust but don't stay any longer than you have to.'

'Thank you,' I said.

'I'm tired now,' she said, lying back on the bed.

'Do you need anything?' I asked.

'No,' she said. 'There's nothing I need.'

I got up and left the hut. Back at our house, everyone was sitting round the kitchen table.

My father was very excited, drumming his fingers on the arm rests of his wheelchair. He asked me what I was going to do.

'I'm leaving now,' I said.

'To join the Wave Singers?' asked my mother, too calmly.

'No,' I said. 'I'm going away.'

'To the Town?' asked my uncle.

'To the Colony?' asked my sister.

'No,' I said. 'I'm going away.'

My father asked me why I was leaving. He said that I couldn't just walk away from the Wave Singing. I really shouldn't make a hasty decision. Besides, Rufus and Goode had come all this way to hear me Sing. I couldn't just go. The least I could do was to stay until they left. Goode was going to have a baby. Maybe she'd like to stay with us for a bit longer, away from the all the bustle in the Town.

I looked around the kitchen.

'Where is Goode?' I asked, coldly.

'In your room,' said my mother.

'Right,' I said.

I went upstairs. Goode was lying on my bed, reading.

'What are you here for?' I asked, curtly.

Goode put the book down and sat up.

'I wanted to thank you,' she said.

'Thank me for what?' I asked.

'For this, of course,' she said, stroking her bump.

'Is it mine?' I asked.

'Whose else could it be?' she said.

'Are you sure?' I asked.

'Of course I'm sure!' she said.

'Why me?' I asked.

'Because I like you,' she said.

'But you barely know me,' I said. 'Why didn't you ask me?'

'What would you have said?' she replied. 'Anyway, you didn't seem exactly unwilling.'

'So what do you want from me?' I said.

'Want from you?' she said. 'I don't want anything from you. You've given me all I've ever wanted.'

'I can't come and live with you,' I said.

'Who's asking you to?' she said.

'I can't be the bairn's father,' I said.

'You are the bairn's father!' she said. 'There's no getting away from it.'

'You know what I mean,' I said.

'No,' she said, 'I don't know what you mean. I've just told you that I'm not expecting anything of you.'

I took my backpack and sleeping bag out of the wall press. Then I began to fill the pack with clothes from the chest at the foot of the bed.

'Are you off to the Fort now?' asked Goode.

'No,' I said.

'Are you going to the Town?' she asked. 'The boat isn't leaving for a couple of days.'

'No,' I said. 'I'm not going to the Town.'

She looked at me sadly.

'Are you going to the Colony?' she asked.

'No,' I said. 'I'm not going to the Colony.'

She looked puzzled.

'Do you know where you're going?' she asked.

'No,' I said. 'Not really.'

'You'll not get very far on that leg,' she said.

'We'll see,' I said.

I closed the chest and turned to leave. She got up and came across to me.

'Don't think badly of me,' she said. 'Children are all we can give of ourselves to the future. Otherwise there's nothing.'

I stood there, frozen; angry and frightened.

'When you've stopped being like this,' she said, 'you know there's always a bite to eat and a bed with us.'

She lay back and took up her book. I slung the backpack over my shoulders.

'What are you reading?' I asked, conversationally.

'*The Green Child*,' she said, curtly.

I went back down stairs. Everyone was quiet. Everyone watched me.

'I'll need some food,' I said.

'Help yourself,' said my mother.

I opened the larder and took out a sack of maize meal.

My father asked me how long I would be gone for. He said that if I was away for too long then the oldest Wave Singer might choose someone else. You'd better take some water as well, said my mother.

I rounded on my mother.

'You set me up, didn't you,' I said to her. 'You and Rufus and Goode.'

'Don't be daft,' said my mother. 'Why would I do that?'

My father asked us what we were talking about.

'Where do you think Goode's bairn came from?' I said.

My father replied that he really didn't care where the baby came from. Babies were always welcome. Without babies there wouldn't be people. Without people there wouldn't be an Ark. Without an Ark we'd all perish in the Great Flood. Without babies there wouldn't be anyone to perish in the Great Flood, said my mother, gently entwining her fingers in his. Take one of the water carriers from the outhouse.

'You both knew what Goode wanted, didn't you,' I challenged my mother and uncle.

My mother looked pointedly at my uncle. My uncle looked sheepish.

'So why didn't you tell me?' I asked him.

'It's all for the best,' said my uncle, distractedly. 'Goode's delighted and I'm sure you'll get used to the idea.'

'Who are you to decide that for me?' I said. 'Don't I have any choice in the matter?'

'Where do choices come from?' asked my mother. 'You didn't have to come to Town with me. You certainly didn't have to go to bed with Goode.'

'But she got into bed with me!' I exclaimed.

'It doesn't really make any difference now, does it,' said my mother. 'You've got more choices than you know what to do with. So choose.'

'I told you,' I said. 'I'm leaving.'

I turned away and made for the front door. My mother got up and followed me outside.

'Don't be angry with me,' she said. 'I'd never do anything that would harm you.'

'You lied to me about finding your Stretch,' I said.

'Yes, I did,' she said. 'I didn't want you to have any expectations. I was wrong.'

'You knew Goode wanted a child,' I said.

'Yes, I did,' she said, 'but I didn't think it was any business of yours. And I certainly didn't know she'd chosen you. You knew that before I did.'

'You won't tell me about the Project,' I said.

'No, I won't,' she said. 'Not yet, anyway.'

'But Goode knows,' I said.

'No she doesn't,' said my mother. 'Don't you think she'd have told you if she did?'

'She said something about trying to escape,' I said.

'And where would we escape to?' said my mother. 'This is all we have. Do you think we'd stay if there was any alternative?'

'You said things would be clearer after the Singing,' I said, 'but they aren't. If anything they're even more confused. Why are you so hard on me?'

'Some one's got to be,' said my mother. 'Look at your father. Look at your uncle. I love them more than I can ever tell. But they're both utterly defeated. I don't want you to be like them.'

'I better be off then,' I said. 'Before it's too late.'

'Why don't you wait until the morning?' said my mother. 'It's dark now. You'll not get very far.'

'No,' I said. 'I've got to go now.'

I took the path out of the Village and up through the dunes onto the moor. The sky was clear and the moon had risen from behind the mountains. Across the moor, I could see lights from the

Colony. I thought that I might say goodbye to the red-headed girl with the large feet. Maybe I could ask her to come with me.

I walked over the moor towards the Colony. As I got nearer I could see the darting flames from a large fire. As I entered the Colony, I could hear the sounds of drums and pipes and see the shadowy forms of dancers. Then I spied the red-headed girl and the red-headed boy, silhouetted against the light from the fire, entwined in each other's arms.

Feeling empty, I turned away and set off towards the hills at the edge of the moor. The path climbed steadily, growing steeper and narrower, rising up to a ridge.

When I reached the top, I stopped and looked back down across the moor. Beyond the Colony, the dry Firth bed twinkled with the house lights from the Villages. I could just make out our Village against the dark form of the Gate. Behind me, the road through the mountains ran along the ridge.

I was sad to leave. I was glad to leave.

The Book of Loss

. . .

coaches

cobras

cocaine

coca cola

cochineal

cochleal implants

cockatoos

cock fighting

cocoa

coconuts

codeine

cod liver oil

coffee

cognac

cold calling

collagen implants

collective bargaining

collective punishment

colostomy bags

combination locks

communion wine

community charges

compound interest

compressed air

computers

concentration camps

concertinas

concrete

concubines

condoms

condominiums

confidence tricksters

confidential files

conger eels

conglomerates

congregations

console games

conspiracy theories

constables

constitutions

consultants

consulates

container lorries

. . .

Inside

10 I followed the road towards the pass into the mountains. The surface was weathered and fractured, but still flat and firm. The moon was high and I could see my way clearly as I entered the pass. Through the pass, the mountains diverged, forming a broad glen. The road wound down to and along the floor of the valley.

I stopped on a piece of level ground by the road and took off my backpack. Then I unrolled my sleeping bag and got into it without undressing. I fell asleep immediately.

When I woke I was wet with dew. I ached all over and my feet hurt. The sun was low behind the mountains and a cold breeze blew down the glen. I stood up, stretched and looked around. The mountains and the valley floor were bare rock that sparkled in the sunlight. Nothing grew and there was no indication that anything had ever grown there.

I began to have second thoughts about my journey. I had no idea what lay ahead. If I ate and drank as I liked, my food and water would last a week at most. I would lose nothing by turning back.

I would gain nothing by turning back. The woman with the brand on her forehead had made it through the mountains without food or water. I knew what lay behind me. Returning would not change why I left.

I took a sip of water and mixed and ate a small bowl of maize meal porridge. When the sun rose over the mountains, I packed up my bag and set off.

As I walked, I thought about the barren lands I was travelling across. Before the Event, the glen must have been a vital link through the mountains. Much of the glen was broad and level enough to support agriculture and there would have been settlements along the road. Now, the glen was uniformly bare. I supposed it had been scoured clean by the Event but I was puzzled as to how the road had survived when everything else had been swept away.

My journey through the glen took much longer than I had expected. As I travelled, I paced myself steadily. If I moved too quickly I would tire myself out. If I moved too slowly I would run out of supplies.

The glen was quiet and still. In the Village there was always the bustle in the background of people coming and going and busying themselves. Especially people talking, almost invariably about each other. On the moor there was solitude but not quiet. The wind whispered in the heather and the sheep called menacingly to each other. But traversing the glen, all I could hear was the beat of my feet and the sound of myself behind my face.

On the morning of the eighth day, the glen narrowed and the road entered another pass that snaked out of the mountains. Towards the foot of the pass, heather and small shrubs began to grow on the flanks of the glen. Beyond the pass, the road entered a broad plain, covered with brush which became denser the further south I travelled.

I tried to keep to the road. I had little sense of how far I had come and I was increasingly anxious that I might lose my way. Apart from the road, there was no sign that anyone had been here before. I had very little water left and always felt thirsty. Without water, the maize was inedible.

I walked for another three days before I reached the shores of the river. The river bed was dry and stony. It would take a lot of work to clear enough ground to grow anything. Another row of hills ran along the far bank of the river. These hills were bare, like the glen I'd just traversed.

I followed the road along the bank, high above the river bed, towards the sea. A further morning's walk brought me to a vantage point looking out along the Firth. In the middle distance, a double row of low, squat stumps marched across the valley. The top of each stump looked smooth and flat, as if the bridge had been snapped clean from its piers.

A kilometre or so before it reached the stumps, the road crossed over a burn; the first running water I had seen since leaving the Village. I quickly left the road, knelt down and drank my fill. The water was cold and sweet. It was a still afternoon and warm in the sun so I took all my clothes off. My body was grey and grimy, I had lost weight and my ribs showed. I crouched in the burn and washed myself all over.

As I eased the tangles out of my hair, a gentle breeze picked up and I heard low, faint, rhythmic sounds coming from downstream. I straightened up and looked around. A little way below where I stood, the burn had been dammed by a rough stone wall. Water spilled over the top. I put on my boots and walked across to the dam. The rhythmic sounds became steadily louder.

I looked over the wall. The land sloped steeply down to the river bed. Beyond the wall, a stone-lined gully carried the water from a spillway down to a house built up against the steep river bank. Steps ran beside the gully. Excited and relieved, I dressed and hurried down the steps.

The house was made of stone and roofed with grey slate tiles.

The gully that bore the burn ran under the wall, through the house. Outside the front door of the house, tubular wind chimes hung from a hook. The door was held shut by a simple wooden latch.

I lifted the latch and entered the house. It was dark inside and smelt damp. The single room was almost bare, save for a rough wooden table and bench. There was a stone fireplace on the wall opposite the door. A chimney breast led up through the ceiling. The gully carried the water into a deep stone-lined trench that ran along the front wall. The room was shelved with stacks of wooden boxes.

At first I was puzzled by the absence of a bed. Then I spotted a curtain hung across the back wall, made from the same furry skins as the coat worn by the woman with the brand on her forehead. I drew the curtain and entered a deep cave that ran back into the river bank.

There was a large bed against the left-hand wall, covered with a blanket of fur. I began to wonder where all the skins came from. I didn't recognise the fur and I had seen no animals since leaving the moor.

As my eyes became used to the gloom, I realised that the walls were rendered smooth with clay, and decorated with elaborate stucco patterns of shells and stones. Along the top of the walls, picked out in flakes of white quartz, was the Wave Singers' motto:

> In the dark times
> Will there also be singing?
> Yes, there will also be singing
> About the dark times.

I went back into the room and inspected the boxes. Most held household goods from before the Event, organised by function and neatly arrayed by size and shape. I began to wonder where all the manufactured goods came from. They were like those from our Town's Store but I had seen no sign of habitation before reaching the house.

I was hungry but there was no food in any of the boxes that I'd checked.

I went back outside and looked around. The burn ran out of the house and curved round through the centre of a market garden into a compound fenced off with chicken wire. Along the far end of the compound was a row of small cages and a low wooden hut. Next to the hut was a large pile of rabbit bones. The bones were fractured and splintered, as though they had been prised open by extremely sharp teeth. The hut was far too big for rabbits. Perhaps whatever had been kept in the hut had been the source of the furs. The gate in the fence was open. Maybe the woman with the brand had released whatever had been kept in the hut before she returned to our Village.

The market garden was well planted with autumn vegetables but overgrown with weeds. At the back of the house was a compost frame and a lean-to shed. Inside the shed was a large stack of kindling and firewood, and a variety of tools and implements. Behind the shed was a wooden box full of rancid animal fat.

I took a spade and a bucket from the shed. Then I stripped back the weeds from the first plot revealing serried rows of potatoes, onions, carrots, spinach and beans. When I had half-filled the bucket with vegetables, I returned to the house and searched the boxes for some means of lighting the fire.

In our Village, every household had a brazier of charcoal in a small stone hut set apart from the house. It was the duty of the oldest child in the household to feed the brazier. If a brazier went out, which happened very rarely, then neighbours would provide embers to restart it. For lighting fires away from the house, on sunny days we would use a burning glass and on wet days we would carry embers.

In a box near the fire place, I found a bow drill. Next to the drill, were a small container of fur and a large tub of fine wood shavings. At school, we had been shown how to start a fire with a drill but I had never needed to use one until now.

I sat cross legged by the fireplace and assembled the drill. Placing one end of the spindle into the depression in the fire board, I pressed the socket down on the other end and started to saw. I remembered that I should press firmly and saw slowly, to produce wispy smoke and fine sawdust. It was hard to maintain an even pace and steady pressure. My hands and arms began to ache.

Eventually, the notch in the fire board filled with wood powder. I decreased the pressure on the spindle and drilled more quickly. Smoke began to pour from the end of the drill. I stopped drilling and blew on the pile of dust. The pile of dust began to smoulder. I blew steadily and fed the glowing dust with fur. When the fur caught fire, I quickly moved it onto a bed of wood shavings and built a pyre of kindling around it. When the kindling caught light, I built up the fire with wood.

There was a large battered saucepan next to the fireplace. I filled it with water and put it onto the metal grill astride two large stones. Then I washed the vegetables in the stream and chopped them fine. When the water came to the boil, I added the vegetables and placed a lid on the saucepan. I went through the boxes again and found bunches of dried plants. Some were herbs that I knew from our Firth but there were others that I didn't recognise. I crushed sage and parsley leaves between my fingers, and stirred the seasoning into the soup.

Hungry and impatient, I took the saucepan off the fire and

filled a mug with soup. The soup had a raw taste and the vegetables were barely soft, but the warmth suffused my body like the Waves of the Song.

It was getting dark and the wind had picked up from the east. I opened the door and peered outside. The wind was chill on my nostrils and smelt of snow. I shut and latched the door. Then I went through to the cave, took my clothes off and got into the bed.

I curled up but I was too tired to sleep. The bed was clammy and the fur rugs felt ticklish against my skin. The wind began to howl in the chimney. I felt very small and alone.

The firelight flickered round the edges of the curtain. I picked up my clothes and the bedding and went back through to the living room. Moving the table away from the fireplace, I banked up the fire, made a mattress from the fur rugs and slipped into my sleeping bag. There was a cold draught where the burn went through the house but it was warm by the fire and I soon fell asleep.

11 Early in the morning I was awakened by a scrabbling noise at the door. The noise was persistent, as if whatever was outside had been used to being let into the house. Alarmed, I sat up and threw my shoe at the door. The scrabbling noise stopped.

Before the Event, people kept animals as pets. They were supposed to be companionable, especially for people who lived alone. Perhaps the woman with the brand had kept one. But pets ate food that people could have eaten.

We had no pets in the Village. Animals were wild and had little affection for people. We bred animals for their flesh and their skin. We tended them with care but we only afforded them as much dignity as their brains warranted.

I lay by the fire until dawn, more awake than asleep. Then I got up, raked over the fire and put the soup on to warm while I washed. After breakfast, I dressed up warmly and shut up the house. Then I walked back up beside the burn to the road and set off towards the stumps of the bridge.

The wind was raw. I knew that I didn't have very much time to explore the hill in the centre of the city before the snows came. But I was worried about whatever had woken me early that morning.

Before the Event, people kept animals in zoos. The animals were often from foreign countries. People paid money to come and look at the animals. Those animals with enough brain to notice their confinement were sullen and listless.

I wondered what had happened to the animals in the zoos

after the Event. Most would have died or been eaten by other animals or human survivors. Perhaps some animals thrived in the new climates of their places of exile.

As I neared the stumps of the bridge, I started to pass low mounds which must once have been houses. The mounds were covered in brambles and gorse and ivy and privet and rose bushes. On the other side of the stumps, the mounds became larger and more frequent. The city was far bigger than the Town at the other end of our Loch. From the sizes of the mounds, many of the buildings in the city would have dwarfed the Town Ark.

The road entered a broad flat area, enclosed by extensive, tall mounds. To the left, a smaller road branched away from the Firth. I took the road up to a plateau at the base of a round hill. The hill was completely surrounded by the city. I tried to imagine it thronged with people. A track wound up the side of the hill.

I climbed the track to the top where I stopped and looked out across the Firth. Beyond the city, I could see another row of stumps from a second bridge. Between the bridges were the lineaments of a settlement like ours.

I wondered why the settlement had been abandoned. Maybe the people had died of starvation or illness. Perhaps they had left in search of better pasture. Maybe the people from the settlement had joined our Village. Perhaps they had founded our Village.

I began to realise how little I knew of our people's history. We were taught all about the Event at school but our teachers were vague about how long ago it had happened. I had always had the impression that the Event was at most two hundred years ago.

In the encyclopaedia, I had seen photographs of ancient Mayan and Toltec temples emerging from tropical rainforest. The overgrown temples looked much like the mounds of the city but they had been at least four hundred years old when the pictures were taken.

On the far side of the hill were more low rectangular mounds surrounding what must have been a substantial cylindrical structure. Their tops were partially exposed, revealing aged, pitted concrete.

I walked aimlessly round and round the mounds. There was no obvious way in to any of them.

In the books my mother read, a whisper of air on a still day might reveal an unexpected opening; an animal might dart into a vent obscured by vegetation; an explorer might fall through the rotten cover of a hidden entrance.

I leant back against one of the mounds. Puzzled by the draught across my ankles, I started as a rabbit shot past me and disappeared between the mound and the circular structure. As I tried to follow the rabbit into the undergrowth, the ground suddenly gave way beneath me and I tumbled down a sloping shaft onto a metallic grill.

The grill was held in place by hinges and sliding bolts. I cautiously righted myself. The grill felt solid. I stood up straight. The shaft was slightly deeper than my reach. There were metal rungs set into the wall of the shaft. I held onto a rung and kicked against the grill. Nothing happened. There were access holes for the bolts. I crouched down and tried to move a bolt. The bolt slid back. I couldn't see anything below me so I moved my weight onto the back of the grill and slid the bolt shut. Then I climbed up out of the shaft.

It was late afternoon when I got back to the house. All day there had been no sign of whatever had woken me that morning. I built up the fire and ate another bowl of soup. Then I found a knife and started to cut a fur rug into long, thin cords. The knife blunted quickly and I rubbed my hands raw.

I knotted cords into three lengths which I plaited together into a rope. Then I tied knots in the rope at regular intervals. When I had finished, the sun had long set but the moon was high. I walked up the side of the burn and inspected the dam. A large natural rock formed one corner. The rock was too heavy for me to lift. I tied one end of the rope around the rock. Then I tied the other end of the rope around my waist and walked backwards down the flank of the dam. When the rope was taut, I leaned back into space. Suspended by the rope, I watched the clouds scudding across the moon.

That night I slept soundly. Early in the morning I was awakened by the scrabbling at the door. I lay quietly and listened. The scrabbling soon stopped and I went back to sleep.

There had been a sharp frost overnight. Purple clouds gathered out over the dry sea bed. I spent the morning in the garden digging up vegetables. After lunch, I bound brushwood lathered with tallow onto a branch. Putting the torch, bow drill, rope and knife into my bag, I walked back to the hill, wary of whatever was waking me so early in the morning.

On top of the hill, I cleared away the bushes from around the top of the shaft, climbed down onto the grill and slid back one bolt. Back up out of the shaft, I lit a fire in the lee of the building and ignited the torch. I returned to the top of the shaft and secured the rope to the top rung. Then I climbed back down the shaft, wedged myself across the grill and slid back the other bolt. The grill fell away and I dropped the torch into the space below. The torch flickered and flared. The floor was a short distance from the grill so I relaxed my grip and landed awkwardly on the rough concrete.

Bruised but unbroken, I picked up the torch and looked

around. The building was completely empty. A steel door led away from one end. I tried the door. It was unlocked so I went through it into another building.

The second building was full of human bones. The light from the torch cast unsettling shadows across the walls and ceiling. Along the walls were neat piles of tibia and fibula, hips and ribs, spines and clavicles. The skulls were arranged in a conical heap in the centre of the building. Many of the long bones had deep, straight, score marks, as if they had been methodically butchered.

I had seen human bones before, though never so many. I was frightened of live things not dead ones.

Before the Event, the dead were buried where nothing useful grew. Since the Event, we can't afford to waste any source of nutrient or energy. In times of plenty, we bury our dead in our poorest pastures and celebrate the first harvests from the fields they enrich.

In times of famine, we eat our dead. Perhaps one winter had been so harsh that the people from the settlement couldn't bury the bones of the dead that they had eaten. Perhaps the people from the settlement had starved to death.

I went past the bones and through another unlocked steel door. The walls of the third building were lined with gutted electronic equipment and bare cabinets. On the far wall, one cabinet was still closed. Inside were rows of manuals, shrink wrapped in tough, transparent polythene.

I had never seen so much polythene before. Polythene was a scarce substance. And transparent polythene was especially prized. Our people would have long consumed the polythene and the manuals. Perhaps the people from the settlement had deemed the manuals too important to reclaim. Maybe they had perished before they could reclaim the manuals.

I browsed the spines of the manuals. They all had the code X-FLR6, just like the cover of my uncle's disk. I read the spines more carefully. Most of the manuals seemed to be concerned with the operating procedures for specific pieces of equipment. One was entitled:

Root Repeater Station to Satellite:
Core Transmission Protocols.

I put the manual in the bag, went back past the bones to the first building, climbed clumsily up the rope, shut and bolted the grill and left the shaft.

Snow had started to fall, small flakes, dancing in the breeze. As I walked back towards the house, the snow flakes grew larger. By the time I reached the stumps, the snow was settling on the mounds and on the road. Beyond the stumps, away from the shelter of the mounds, the wind grew stronger and the snow grew thicker. As I neared the house, I could barely see the road. By the time I reached the house, my chest and thighs were caked with snow and my face and ears burnt with the cold.

I brushed myself down and went into the house. The fire had gone out. The house was very cold. I gathered up an armful of firewood from the shed and re-lit the fire. Then I wrapped myself in a fur rug, sat by the fire and carefully opened the manual.

The manual was incomprehensible. I understood most of the words separately but they made no sense together. The pages were larded with unexplained acronyms. Footnotes referred to other manuals that were probably still in the building. The manual would have furnished my father with plenty of arkles.

I felt extraordinarily tired. I heated and drank the rest of the soup. Then I went to bed by the fire.

Early in the morning, I was awakened by the scrabbling at the door. I lay quietly until the scrabbling stopped. Then I got up and opened the door. Strange footprints led away from the door across the snow. Each footprint was shaped like a hand.

I thought about following the footprints but the snow was still falling heavily and had started to blow into the house. I shut the door, put more wood on the fire and went back to bed.

By the time I got up, the snow had covered the strange footprints. The woman with the brand had told me to leave before the snows came. I hadn't asked her how long the snows lasted.

12 I spent the morning moving all the wood from the shed into the cave, and the afternoon digging up the rest of the vegetables from the kitchen garden.

That evening, I tried to read the manual more systematically. Communication with the satellites seemed to be based on layers of messages. To begin with, very simple sequences of basic control signals had to be sent to initiate more complex communication at the next levels. The sequences of signals were described using ideas that I didn't understand. The manual was not supposed to be read on its own by someone who didn't know anything about the X-FLR6 programme.

In desperation, I turned to the appendices. The first appendix listed all the basic control signals, with terse explanations of what they did. The second appendix had tables showing how each basic control signal was represented in binary. The last appendix contained what was called the Primary Startup Sequence. This consisted of several dozen lists of binary codes. Alternate lists were marked 'Repeater' or 'Satellite'. Perhaps I could use the tables to translate the code lists back into sequences of basic control signals.

I sharpened the end of a twig and charred it in the fire. Then I carefully tore out a blank piece of paper from the back of the manual and copied the first list of binary codes from the Primary Startup Sequence in a column down the left side of the page. As I wrote, I began to recognise regular patterns of codes. When I'd finished, I looked up each code in the tables in the second appendix and wrote the equivalent basic control signal next to it. Finally, I looked up each signal in turn in the first appendix and wrote down its explanation next to it. Some signals were followed by sequences of untranslatable binary codes.

At the end of the list, I read the sequence of explanations:

```
message starts
from: <root repeater station identification next 4 bytes>
00010001 00010001 00010001 00010001
from: <root operator identification next 4 bytes>
10101010 10101010 10101010 10101010
to: <root satellite identification next 4 bytes>
01010101 01010101 01010101 01010101
request: global reset
request: root initialisation
request: status
message ends
```

I repeated the process with the second list. Again, I began to recognise patterns of codes, some of which had appeared in the first list. The sequence of explanations for the second list read:

```
message starts
from: <root satellite identification next 4 bytes>
01010101 01010101 01010101 01010101
to: <root repeater station identification next 4 bytes>
00010001 00010001 00010001 00010001
to: <root operator identification next 4 bytes>
10101010 10101010 10101010 10101010
response: acknowledge global reset
response: global reset successful
response: acknowledge root initialisation
response: root initialisation successful
response: acknowledge request status
response: ready
response: stand-by
request: action
message ends
```

I read both lists of explanations again and again. I could see requests and responses but I couldn't understand what had been requested or what had been responded. I didn't think that I could make any further progress without reading more of the X-FLR6 manuals.

The fire was low and my head ached. I built up the fire and went to bed.

Early in the morning, I was awakened by the scrabbling at the door. When the scrabbling stopped, I got up and opened the door. There was nothing there. I shut the door and went back to bed.

The next day, I wrapped myself up in a fur rug and set off for the ruined city. As I came closer, the snow drifts became deeper and deeper. When the snow reached up to my thighs, I returned to the house.

I spent the rest of the day indoors. I made more soup and deciphered more of the messages. The messages all had the same structure of identifications, requests and responses. As I deciphered them, I realised that I was humming to myself.

Before I left our Village, I could have joined the Wave Singers; since I'd left I hadn't Sung or even thought about the Song. I had thought a lot about staying alive. And I had thought a lot about the red-headed girl with the large feet. Mostly though, all I'd thought about was finding explanations for the noises I'd heard on the Colonist's radio and my uncle's disk.

I stopped deciphering the messages and tried to clear my mind for the Song. The Song wouldn't come. I tried to feel the Song within my body. The Song wasn't there. I tried to ignore the Song. The Song still ignored me.

The fire was low and my head was empty. I built up the fire and went to bed.

Early in the morning, I was awakened by the scrabbling at the door. I quickly got up and opened the door. A short, vague form disappeared into the darkness. I shut the door and returned to bed.

The next day, the snow on the dry Firth had started to melt. I wrapped myself up in a fur rug and walked through the soft snow to the settlement between the bridges.

The settlement was larger than our Village but smaller than our Town. The buildings had been laid out in neat rows. I walked down one side of the settlement, towards the mouth of the Firth. The buildings were all tumbled down and overgrown. There had been enough houses for several hundred people. I couldn't tell for how long it had been abandoned. I carried on through the settlement until I reached the remains of the second bridge. Like the first bridge, it appeared to have been broken cleanly from its piers. The stumps of the two central piers looked much larger than the others, as if they had been extended to form Gates like those at the boundary of our Village.

Just beyond the second bridge, I crossed a well-worn path which led across the Firth to the opposite bank from the ruined city. In the snow along the path were many footprints like those in the snow outside the house by the burn. I re-crossed the path and walked back through the middle of the settlement. In the centre were the remains of an Ark. The Ark had been much larger than my father's.

I wondered about the people who had lived in the settlement. Were they like us? Did they Sing or were they before Singing? The people in the settlement had built Gates and an Ark. Were there Gates and Arks before there was Singing? Did people build Gates and Arks before the Event? Did they Sing before the Event?

It was late afternoon and the slushy snow was beginning to freeze over. I left the settlement and returned to the house.

I was hungry. I hadn't eaten since I'd got up. I was growing tired of the taste of the vegetable soup. I inspected the boxes that I hadn't looked at before, trying to find something else with which to flavour the vegetables. One box was full to the brim with crumbly green leaves, which smelt faintly aromatic but musty, as if they had been in the box for a long time. I boiled some water and made an infusion with the leaves. The infusion smelt pungent but not unpleasant. I tried a sip: it tasted curiously familiar. I drank a cup of the infusion. It warmed me up but I still felt hungry.

I decided to try to bake some vegetables. I raked the fire, placed three potatoes in the hot ashes and balanced an onion on top of them. Then I lay back on the bed and gazed vacantly into the embers.

The embers glowed red, and dulled again as the draught from the burn played across them. Gazing into the embers I felt very peaceful and my mind slowly emptied of all thoughts of where I'd come from and where I was. Languidly, I closed my eyes and watched the soft-coloured shapes playing across my field of view. The shapes became sharper and the colours became brighter. The shapes, framed in black and gold, whirled round and round, faster and faster, in kaleidoscope swirls.

I began to feel dizzy and opened my eyes. I was still lying by the fire. I sat up and prodded the potatoes. The potatoes still felt firm. I lay back down and shut my eyes.

The swirls spiralled into a deep, dark tunnel of peristaltic rings of rainbow teardrops, tumbling away into a bright nothingness. The teardrops flowed through each other, stretching and flattening into rippling tessellations of twisting polygons. As each polygon struck the centre of the tunnel it burst, sounding a pure, bright note. At first the notes clashed discordantly, one against the next. Then the polygons began to align themselves into long ribbons

115

that streamed down the sinuous walls of the tunnel. The polygons glowed in constantly changing shades, bursting resonantly in tuneless tones as they hit the tunnel's end. The colours steadily muted and the shapes shrank until each ribbon was formed solely of pulsating light and dark triangles of green, red and blue. The light triangles burst silently but the dark triangles all sounded the same high, clear note. The ribbons circled each other in intertwined helices, taking it in turns to shed their next triangle. The ribbons streamed faster and faster and the individual notes melded into a continuous sound that rose higher and higher. As I listened intently to the bursting triangles, I began to hear, deep in my mind, the noise from the Colonists' radio and my uncle's disk. As I stared intently at the ribbons, I suddenly saw, deep in my mind, the streams of bytes from the communications manual.

I smelt burning and sat up. The potatoes and the onion were smouldering. I was very hungry. I fished the potatoes and onion out of the fire onto a plate and prised away their blackened outer skins. Then I mashed the onion into the potato with a little water and quickly ate the thick, steaming pottage.

Replete, I lay on my back and shut my eyes but the swirling shapes had faded away. I opened my eyes and vacantly watched the shadows playing on the ceiling.

I felt strangely elated. I didn't need to understand the Primary Startup Sequence or fetch any more manuals from the building on the hill. If I could read the lists of binary codes as music then I could whistle them to the satellite, just as the girl with the red hair and the large feet had suggested.

I felt strangely sad. I realised that I didn't care about the satellite. I cared about the girl with the red hair but I knew she didn't care about me.

I got up and went outside. The speckled sky glowed crimson in the setting sun. The sun was setting earlier and earlier each day. Soon it would be mid-winter and Kropotkin's Birthday. As I watched the sunset, I thought about my household and how this would be the first Kropotkin's Birthday I'd spent without them.

As I watched the sunset, I felt the Song welling up inside me. I threw back my head and arms and Sang to the sunset, harsh and desperate, until the sun disappeared beyond the dry Firth. Exhausted, I went indoors, banked up the fire and got into bed.

Early in the morning, I was awakened by the scrabbling at the door. Washed out and utterly indifferent, I turned over and went back to sleep.

Andrew

It's my turn to cook. It feels like it's always my turn since the boy went away.

I do miss the boy. I hope he's all right, wherever he is. I don't think she really wanted him to go. Latterly, she was a bit hard on him. She meant well though.

I don't have much clue what to make. I always seem to make the same things, over and over again. She'd tell me to look through the recipe books for ideas, but they're not much use. There are so many ingredients we don't have any more.

I'll maybe just finish another couple of Arkles before I start cooking. I still don't really understand why she was so pissed off with me for using the blank pages. It's not as if there were any words on them.

I'm still astonished that she chose me. She could have had anyone. Others were so much better with words. Now words seem almost all that matter to her.

That's unfair.

I suppose I could make some tortillas. For a change, the boy would say. He was quite a decent cook. Always consistent if not very imaginative. A bit like me. I could always make dumplings.

The maize is running low. Maybe we can trade some beetroot. There's always too much beetroot.

My fingers are seizing up again. It would be so

much easier to make bigger Arkles but the Arkist said that they wouldn't give enough buoyancy. Besides, making them as small as possible is supposed to help the meditation.

I wonder what it would be like to eat an orange. What it would it taste of.

Whenever I try to clear my mind, to be at one with the Ark, the last remnants are still lurking there. I'm sure she still remembers.

If I can get the food in the oven fairly soon then I should have time to visit the Ark before she gets back. I know she doesn't like me going. She never says anything though.

I do wonder why she chose me. She was so bright. All the boys fancied her. Especially me but I thought I'd have no chance there. She was sharp with her tongue though. That put them off.

It was Kropotkin's Birthday. She was sitting by herself, nose in a book as always. I was across the hall from her. Everyone else was dancing. Yes, I was watching her. Whenever anyone approached her she glanced up and glared at them. Maybe they thought she looked defiant. I thought she looked lonely. What had I to lose?

When I asked her to dance, she put down her book and smiled at me. It wasn't until much later that I realised how short sighted she was.

I wish people weren't sorry for me. The fall redeemed me. She was so angry when I first suggested it.

I wonder what curry would taste like. So many strange ingredients. Coconut. Coriander. Cumin. Turmeric. Ginger. Lemon juice. Pepper. Cardamom. Chilli. All just words now.

The Arkist says we make our own futures. Everything's connected and everything balances.

It's all in The Book of the Ark.

The weans will soon be home from school. Just one more Arkle. This feels like a promising leaf. Fibrous but not too brittle…

I was high on the tower, leaning into the breeze. The wind changed and I braced myself as the mill turned. But the tower leant further and further away and I heard the spars scream as they started to fracture. Suddenly everything was still and I was falling free.

I took forever to fall. As I fell, I watched myself again that awful night, taking the bairn from her and setting out across the frozen fields. Beyond the Gates, I could see the low forms against the moonlit plain. I held the bairn close but she wouldn't stop greeting. And I felt a sickening dread at what we had done and what I was about to do.

I was still falling, oh so slowly, the shattered spars twisting and turning all around me.

As I went through the Gates, I heard a weak voice calling:

'Over here! Over here!'

I followed the calls to the huddle of bodies against the wall.

'Who's there?' I asked, sad beyond endurance. I knew fine who was there. I had recognised the voice.
'Who are you?' asked my old teacher.
'It's Andrew from The Village,' I replied.
'Have you brought your child?' she said. 'Give her here. It's so cold. We'll both sleep soon.'

And as I gently laid our daughter down into my dying teacher's arms, everything speeded up and I felt suddenly at peace as I crashed into the platform.

I was badly concussed and I'd broken both hips. They said I was lucky not to break my spine. It was agony every time they moved me. It was clear even then that I'd never support myself unaided.

I spent a year in bed, pissing and shitting myself, before they'd let me even try to sit up. But she looked after me. And it still all works just fine under the kilt.

The Arkist said that it was my fate to fall. That made her so cross. But it made good sense to me. Fate isn't the same as fault.

Still, The Book of the Ark is a puzzle. The Arkist says it teaches us how to live with forces we can't fathom. The Great Flood is an inevitability that we must all be prepared for. But it's obvious that the Ark would never float even if it were stuffed full of Arkles. I'm sure we could build a floating Ark. I bet Rufus could design one.

Poor Rufus. I know he blames himself for my fall. I'll never blame him for anything except making me believe that things could be other than they are. Anyway, I mostly did that to myself.

I'd never been so happy as when we were building the high tower. We'd had good harvests year on year. The weans were blossoming. Even then I could tell that the boy was going to be a fine Singer. And she seemed to be coming back out of herself at last.

High on the tower, I could look out over the Village and see them all far below. I felt like their guardian angel. If only I'd had wings.

I knew that if I could just build the tower that bit higher, then the sails might find the currents where the kites soared, and if I kept them trim they'd turn so steady. I was a fool.

That's the weans coming along the boardwalk. And I've not even started to cook yet. I wonder what homework they've got. I can't be doing with arithmetic. It's funny that she's no use at arithmetic either.

I shouldn't have made that last Arkle. If I don't get the food on soon I'll not have time to get to the Ark and back.

Still, maybe I could trundle myself along to the midden after we've eaten. She doesn't like that much either.

I'll need to get one of the weans to have a look at the chair. The wheels have started to squeak again. Lard's best for them but it goes off so quickly…

13 It snowed on and off for the next few weeks. I spent most of my time indoors, pouring over the lists of binary code. I tried to whistle the codes as I read them, pausing for the noughts and trilling the ones, but I couldn't whistle fast enough to run the trills and pauses together into the satellite music. I tried to whistle the sounds from the radio and disk as I read the codes, but I couldn't read the codes quickly enough, or whistle the sounds slowly enough, for them to merge. I tried drinking more of the infusion, but it made me dozy and introspective. In my mind, I tried to hear the satellite music as I watched the codes, but all I could see were the ones and noughts, and all I could hear was the silence around me.

One morning, after I was awakened by the scrabbling at the door, I lay in bed and thought about food. I was tired of eating nothing but vegetables. I hadn't eaten meat for many weeks. The woman with the brand had talked about catching rabbits. I had seen a rabbit on the hill in the city. I wondered if any rabbits living nearer to the house had survived the poisoned dust. If there weren't any rabbits nearby, perhaps I could cage and eat whatever woke me each morning.

I went outside as soon as it was light. The footprints in the snow approached the door from the burn and continued away across the dry Firth to the hills beyond. I followed the footprints back up to the burn. Just beyond the dam, the snow had been churned into mud at the water's edge. In the mud were rabbit prints running up along the bank. I followed the rabbit prints back to an extensive warren above the road from the glen.

I returned to the house and un-twined a dozen cords from the rope. I scraped the fur from the cords and soaked them in water to soften them. Tensioning the cords against the door latch, I twisted and stretched them tight. Then I fashioned nooses and tied each one to a sharpened branch.

Late that afternoon, I returned to the rabbit warren. Some of the burrows had fresh prints at their entrances. I set a trap outside each busy burrow and drove a sharpened branch deep into the earth. Then I laid the noose wide across the burrow's entrance and covered it lightly with snow.

That evening, as I ate vegetable soup, I thought about my lot. It was all of my own making. No one had forced me to leave the safety of our Village for the harsh uncertainties across the mountains. At least I had found the codes and now knew how they were linked to the sounds from the radio and the disk.

But I was tired of trying to hear the codes. I knew that I could do nothing further on my own. I was tired of solitude but I had to stay where I was until the snows finally melted. There was plenty of fuel so maybe, with care, I could eke out the vegetables if I could catch rabbits.

The next morning, I walked back up to the rabbit warren. There were dead rabbits in three of the traps. Each rabbit's coat was caked in blood and its belly had been gnawed away.

I took the rabbits and the traps back down to the house. Then I skinned and cleaned and boned the rabbits and made a large pot of stew. While the stew was cooking, I scraped all the fat off the skins and put it aside for cooking and soap and lighting. Then I hung the skins in the shed to cure and dumped what remained of the rabbits on the compost heap.

The rabbit and vegetable stew tasted very good.

When I'd finished eating, I thought about Singing. Before I left our Village, I had enjoyed Singing. I had Sung well. I had found my Stretch. Perhaps I could find my Stretch again, no matter what the oldest Wave Singer had said.

But after my last long break from Singing, I had Sung very poorly when I'd started again on the full Song. Then I had the discipline of our choir and the structure of our Song to guide me. This time, I had to make my own discipline and structure.

I shaped my days around my Singing. I began with the basic exercises, repeating them over and over again until they became first nature. Then I started working through the Corner Songs to the Island Song. As my Singing grew, I could feel the Song calling to me, urging me to set it free. But I kept the Song captive within me, tantalising it and tormenting it, as I Sang the Island Song against myself.

I shaped my Singing around my days. As the days passed, I watched the moon wax and wane, once, twice, three times. As the days grew shorter and shorter, my Singing grew increasingly confident.

As mid-winter approached, it snowed more frequently and more persistently. One morning, when I awoke, I realised that I hadn't been stirred by the scrabbling at the door. When I got up, I couldn't open the door. I leant heavily against the door but it barely gave. Panicking, I charged at the door and threw my weight against it. The top slats of the door broke free and I fell out into a bank of snow.

I was encased in snow. I couldn't tell how high or deep it had drifted. I desperately hauled myself up by the broken door and climbed back into the house. Flurries of snow tumbled in behind me. I extricated the slats and tried to fit them back into position but they kept falling out into the drift. The house was steadily growing colder. I took down the curtain that divided off the cave and hung it over the door. Then I added the slats to the dwindling wood pile.

The next few days passed very slowly. On that first day, I tried to dig myself out but soon gave up; exhausted, chilled and soaked in sweat. I spent the rest of that day huddled listlessly by the fire. I was desperately worried that I might freeze or starve to death but I was even more frightened by a sudden, deep self-doubt. Even if I survived the winter, how would I get back across the mountains? Even if I returned safely to our Firth, how would I face the red-haired girl?

The following morning, the inside of the house had become dank and stale. I got up and checked behind the curtain. The wall of snow had frozen over night. I tried to chip away at the ice but I made little impact. I went back to bed and lay in the gloom, my thoughts wandering, immersed in my own hopelessness, drowning in self-pity.

Our parents were quintessential survivors. One a dreamer, the other a weaver of dreams, they both taught us to listen to the small clear voice that tells each of us how things are and how they might be.

That evening, I began to remember the stories my father liked to tell. Tales of unforeseen but foreseeable adversity. Tales of travellers reduced to eating their boots. Tales of explorers reduced to eating each other. Tales of adventurers starving to death within walking distance of food. My father was sombre as he told these stories. He said that such people would make very poor Arkists. Anyone who didn't expect the worst probably deserved it. If you didn't prepare to survive, you'd certainly perish when the Great Flood came. There are some things you just can't prepare for, said my mother patiently, massaging embrocation into his shoulders.

The next morning, the doorway was still shrouded in ice, but I felt calmer and less sorry for myself. I tidied the house and made a fresh pot of soup. While the soup was cooking, I Sang the Island Song. When the soup was ready, I ate my fill. Then I stood in the centre of the house and cautiously Sang my Stretch.

When I'd finished Singing, I lay back on the bed. I had enjoyed Singing my Stretch but I knew it had been an icy perfection, and that my enjoyment was mostly relief. Then I thought about the day that I'd found my Stretch and remembered how the oldest Wave Singer had levitated a coin with a rising note that vanished away into silence.

My mother had a small collection of books that she called science fantasy. They seemed to consist of little science and too much fantasy, with plots just like those in historical romances, cowboy stories and detective fiction. In science fantasy books, people who could manipulate objects at a distance either had a genetic mutation that made them telekinetic or they used magic. I thought that both telekinesis and magic were most unsatisfactory bases for fantasy or science.

When I had first started to learn how to Sing, we had spent many lessons practising continuous scales. Our teacher had accompanied us on a Swanee whistle, sliding slowly from each note to the next. Once, one of the choir had asked our teacher what would happen if they continued to sing higher and higher. Our teacher laughed and told us that it wasn't possible to sing beyond a certain limit. He asked us all to sing an ascending scale in unison until we could sing no higher. I was the last to stop, long after the others. Our teacher had looked at me strangely before continuing the lesson.

I knew that anyone could move light objects by blowing at

them hard enough. Sound was essentially vibrating blowing. In the encyclopaedia, I had read about trained singers who could shatter drinking glasses with their voices. Perhaps I could manipulate objects by singing at them silently and shaping the silent sound.

I stood up and sang an ascending scale, higher and higher until I felt my voice straining in my throat. I stopped singing. I was worried that I might damage my voice. I could still hear myself singing at the point when I stopped. I hadn't sung high enough.

After a short break I tried again. This time I sang more slowly and managed to reach further up the endlessly rising scale before I stopped. The higher I sang, the harder it became to hold each note pure and the more my throat began to wobble uncontrollably.

When I was young I had been fascinated by flight. Although we no longer hunted them, the few remaining birds shunned human settlements. I very rarely saw birds flying and always stopped what I was doing to watch them. I had poured over articles in the encyclopaedia about aircraft and helicopters, but I couldn't imagine travelling faster than I could run.

In the encyclopaedia I had read about attempts to break the sound barrier, long before the Event. When an aircraft approached the speed of sound, it began to vibrate violently. As it passed the speed of sound, it quickly settled back into smooth flight. Perhaps my throat was like an aircraft approaching the speed of sound. If I could sing into silence then maybe my throat would settle back into pure notes.

I relaxed my body and started to sing, softly and steadily. As the scale rose, I increased the strength of my singing, fighting against the increasing tremor. As the scale rose, I could feel the chords straining deep in my throat. Suddenly, my throat relaxed and I could no longer hear the notes. There was a loud sharp noise behind me. I stopped singing and threw back the curtain. A deep crack had formed across the centre of the ice that covered the doorway.

I was incredulous. It seemed most unlikely that my voice had cracked the ice. Perhaps the ice had started to thaw and a strong gust of wind had buffeted the house. But I had sung beyond sound. Maybe I could sustain the soundlessness if I could pass more quickly from song to silence.

My throat felt tender. I took a long draught of water from the pan on the fire. Then I took a deep breath and began to sing once more. This time, I moved rapidly up the scale. When my voice fell silent I could still feel my throat vibrating. Cautiously holding the impossibly high note, I swept the silence across the doorway. The ice in the doorway shimmered and shattered, as if it had been struck by a thousand tiny hammers. Then my breath gave out and my voice fell still.

My throat felt battered and sore. I decided not to sing any more that day. I warmed up some soup and tried to eat but my throat throbbed raw with each mouthful I swallowed.

That night I couldn't get to sleep for the sharp pain. In desperation, I made myself a strong infusion of the dried green plant, which soothed my throat and drowsed my mind.

14 The next morning, I was wakened by the scrabbling noise at the door. When I got up, the floor was covered in water. Overnight, the ice and snow had begun to melt.

My throat felt very bad. When I had strained my voice before, my father had dosed me with a concoction of honey and sake from the Colony. Now I had no medicines apart from the green infusion.

I decided that I had to leave as soon as I could. Before I left I had to prepare as much food as I could carry and make fast the house: it had been my refuge and someone else might chance this way.

That morning, I swept out the water and patched up the door. That afternoon, I set the rabbit traps up by the burrows. After supper, I heated a length of copper pipe red hot in the fire and burnt the Sail Tenders' motto into the back of the door:

> *Were a wind to arise*
> *I could put up a sail*
> *Were there no sail*
> *I'd make one of canvas and sticks*

The following day, I went up to the traps and found six rabbits, all with their bellies torn out. I skinned and gutted the rabbits. Then I built up the fire with damp wood and hung up long strips of meat to cure in the hot smoke.

I dug over the vegetable garden, removed the remaining dead growth and added fresh compost from the bottom of the heap. Then I sowed neat rows of seeds from the boxes in the house. Some of the remaining potatoes had started to sprout: as the sun went down, I planted them out.

The last day, I cleaned out the fireplace and tidied up the house and grounds. Then I carefully wrapped the X-FLR6 manual up in its polythene cover and put it in the bottom of my backpack. As well as the manual, I packed the remaining food, the fire drill, a knife, a can, the dried green plants, some kindling and my sleeping bag. Finally, I filled up the water carrier I'd brought from the village. Cloaking myself in a fur rug against the cold, I latched the house, shouldered the backpack and water carrier and set off.

I had thought for some time about which route to take back to the Village. Although the snow and ice had melted in the Firth, the long, bare pass through the mountains might still be impassable. Instead, I set off down the Firth, across the abandoned settlement and out beyond the second bridge.

As I walked into the widening mouth of the Firth, I didn't once stop and look back. I had found what I had come to find and I was anxious to leave. I needed human company and comfortable, easy noise and bustle; to tell people about where I'd been and what I'd found. I wanted to Sing with the choir and to learn more from the oldest Wave Singer about silent singing. I yearned to show the girl with the red hair the X-FLR6 manual and explain how we might use it to talk to the satellite.

I also wanted to ask lots of questions of my parents and my uncle and the woman with the brand on her forehead. How long ago was the Event? Why did we live on our Firth instead of this one? What had become of the people from the abandoned settlement? What were the creatures that woke me each morning? What was the Project?

Beyond the mouth of the Firth, the sea bed was flat. I knew that if I followed the coast, keeping the cliffs to my left, I would eventually come to our Firth.

Each day I walked steadily for nine or ten hours, resting briefly every hour, with a longer break at noon. The days were clear and the nights were cold. Every evening, I lit a small fire and made a thin broth of vegetables and dried rabbit. Then I slept under the stars in my sleeping bag, swathed in the fur rug.

On the first day, as I walked, I sang the songs I'd learnt as a child.

> *I know where I'm going.*
> *I know who's going with me.*
> *I know who I love.*
> *But the deil knows who I'll marry. . .*

In the books my mother read, marriage involved two people living together, generally to the exclusion of other people. Of course, people mostly found this intolerable. In our community, people lived together, or not, as they chose.

That evening, my throat throbbed from the singing.

On the second day, as the light was fading, I came to a small stream. Nothing grew by the stream. The sea bed through which it ran was dry and hard. I washed myself and topped up the water carrier.

In the books my mother read, marriage seemed to involve the transfer of ownership of the woman from her father to her husband. In our community, nobody owned anybody apart from themselves. I was still puzzled by my uncle's suggestion that there might be appropriate ways for people to use each other.

I didn't sing at all that day.

On the third day, towards midday, I came to an immense rift in the dry sea bed. I stood at the edge of the rift and peered into its depths. The walls of the rift were sheer. I could see no way down.

In the books my mother read, people mostly got married to

transfer wealth from the woman's father's family to the woman's husband's family. In our community, we didn't have any wealth. Anybody could use anything if they could justify its use.

That evening, as I set up camp, I gently practised the basic scales. My voice rang true but any sustained volume soon hurt.

On the fourth day, I walked back along the edge of the rift towards the cliffs. At the base of the cliffs the rift suddenly stopped. I made my way slowly up the cliff face, along the side of a steep slope of scree. At the top of the cliffs I stopped and looked down across the dry sea bed. The rift ran straight and broad, away to the horizon.

In the books my mother read, people often got married if the woman became pregnant. It generally didn't seem to matter who the child's father was. In our community, people had obligations to their children but that didn't necessarily involve the parents living together. I certainly didn't want to live with Goode, even if I were her child's father.

That evening, before going to bed, I returned to the simplest scale. During the snows, I had hurt my throat by straining to sing beyond sound. Perhaps my mistake lay in the force with which I sang. This time, as the notes rose, I reduced rather than increasing the force of my singing. My throat barely trembled as I slipped into silence. I sang the scale to silence again and again. Each time, the shade to soundlessness became easier.

On the fifth day, I walked along the cliff top. Beside the cliff top was moor land, covered in heather. Way beyond the moor were the mountains I had walked through when I left our Village. I thought about trying to find a way across the mountains back into the long winding pass that led to our Firth. I knew I would make poor time on the rougher, boggy ground. I followed the cliff top to the far side of the rift and then I clambered back down to the dry sea bed.

In the books my mother read, people often got married because they were in love with each other. This invariably made them unhappy. In the books my mother read, people who loved each other were often unable to marry. This invariably made them unhappy. In our community, expediency was the only basis for forming, or living in, households.

That evening, after I had eaten, I unwrapped the X-FLR6 manual and tore out the remaining bare page. Then I tore the page in half, and a half in half again, and a quarter in half again, and an eighth in half again. I folded a sixteenth of the page into a small, perfectly symmetrical arkle which I placed on the palm of my hand. I raised my palm in front of my mouth and began to sing the scale to silence, focusing the diminishing force of my song onto the arkle. Just as my voice vanished, the tiny arkle rose unsteadily from my palm. I practised the soft scale over and over until I could hold the arkle, hovering in front of me, for as long as I could hold the silent song.

On the sixth day, late in the morning, I rounded a headland and saw a low serrated form some distance ahead of me. As I approached the form, I realised it was the great skeleton of a ship, resting upside down on the dry sea bed. The exposed metal ribs arced across the hull, like a vast toast rack. If such an enormous ship could not survive the Event, there was little hope for even the most skilled of Arkists when the Great Flood came.

All this while, I saw no sign that anyone had ever been here before. There were no remains of habitation; neither pre-Event towns nor post-Event settlements. Until the woman with the brand on her forehead returned to our Village, no one had ever talked about what lay beyond our Firth. Now I found it hard to believe that I was the first person to venture this way.

That evening, I folded an eighth of the torn blank page into a larger arkle. I was tempted to sing with more force, but I feared for my fragile voice. Instead, I moved my palm much nearer to my mouth and sang higher up the silent scale. Eventually, I found a placing for a note that would lift the larger arkle.

On the seventh day, I rounded another headland. Way across the dry sea bed a low shoreline came into view. I had entered another Firth: I hoped it was ours.

Late that afternoon, as I was making camp, the wind rose from up the Firth. The wind bore the smell of burning peat.

That evening, I folded a quarter of the torn blank page into the size of arkle my father favoured. I had to position the arkle very close to my mouth and sing until I was nearly out of breath, before I could finally lift it. I knew there had to be a limit to what I could lift, and for how long, but the quarter-page arkle weighed little compared with the coin that the oldest Wave Singer had raised.

On the eighth day, when I stopped for a break mid-afternoon, I looked back down the Firth and saw that I was close to the place where I'd first tried to find my Stretch.

I felt relieved to be so near to my home. I was elated to be returning with some hope for our future but I felt frightened that my future would be the same as my past. In my heart I knew that I was good for little in our community. I could Sing, but what use was Singing? Perhaps I should have stayed in solitude.

But I had now spent long enough by myself to know that I needed to be amongst people. I wanted to see my parents and my siblings and my uncle and my cousins. I especially wanted to see the girl with the red hair and the large feet.

The sun was setting behind the mountains when I reached the rough stone wall at the boundary of our fields. I followed the wall to the stile and climbed over it onto the path that led back to the Gate. The fields had been recently ploughed, ready for planting, but there was no one else around.

I realised that I hadn't kept proper track of how long I'd been away. I had left on the night of the Autumn Singing. Perhaps today was the Spring Singing and everybody was up on the Gate. I could have been up on the South Gate with my family, hauling on the capstan. I might have been on the Wave Singers' platform, Singing as the Gates swung into place. I had always thought that the Song of the Wave Singers gave us rhythm as we turned the windlass. Now I wondered if their Song actually moved the Gates.

It was nearly dark when I reached the far wall of the Fort. I went through the Gate and turned left along the South Dyke until I reached the midden. There was a light inside the midden hut. I knocked on the hut door.

15

'Who's there?' called the woman with the brand on her forehead.

'It's me,' I said. 'Can I come in?'

'No one's stopping you,' she said. 'The door's open.'

The hut was much cosier than when I had last visited. The woman had fashioned a stove from a rusted iron oil drum and lit the room with tallow lamps made from tins wicked with wool. I was not surprised. Her ingenuity had kept me alive through the winter.

The woman was sitting on her bed, much as I'd left her last autumn.

'Have a seat,' she said, proffering me the woven frame chair. 'I haven't seen you for quite a while.'

'I've brought you something,' I said, taking off the fur I'd wrapped myself in and passing it to her.

She took the fur from me and laid it across her knees.

'You found the house then,' she said. 'I hoped you might.'

'I wanted to thank you,' I said. 'If it wasn't for you, I'd probably be dead.'

She laughed sardonically.

'Don't be so melodramatic,' she said. 'That's what we're all good at, isn't it, surviving.'

I reached into my bag and took out the dried plants.

'I brought you these as well,' I said.

'Thank you,' she said, 'but I don't want them. I'd have brought them with me if I had. I've spent long enough feeling numb. I hope you planted more for whoever winds up there next, though.'

'I planted all the seeds,' I said, 'and the potatoes that I didn't eat.'

'Good,' she said. 'Good. Though I hope no one ever needs them.'

'While you were there, did you ever see anybody else?' I asked her.

'No,' she said. 'Nobody.'

'Nor did I,' I said.

'How did you get back?' she asked me.

'I followed the coast,' I said.

'I tried that once,' she said, 'but I gave up at the chasm. How did you get across?'

'I climbed the cliffs,' I said.

'I thought about that but I was just too tired,' she said.

'Did ever you go any further afield?' I asked.

'Sometimes I went up into the hills across the Firth,' she said, 'but they're bare like the pass through the mountains. Anyway, did you find what you were looking for?'

I told her how I'd stumbled on the entrance to the communications centre and I showed her the X-FLR6 manual but she didn't seem very interested. As I talked, she sat quietly, staring at the rug and stroking it.

'So where did the furs come from?' I asked her, finally.

'Didn't you see them?' she asked me.

'No,' I said. 'Just their foot prints in the snow.'

'They're very shy,' she said, 'and very fierce. When I cleared and planted the garden, the seedlings attracted the rabbits, so I caught some and started to breed them. One morning, I went out to feed the rabbits and found half of them dead with their guts torn away. At first I was really frightened. Then I was really angry. I

142

dug a deep pit in front of the rabbit hutches and covered it with branches. In the night I heard something crashing into the pit. The next morning I found I'd trapped two of them. I left them in the pit without food or water until they stopped snarling.'

'You built the low hut for them,' I said.

'Yes,' she said. 'Over time, they became quite tame, so long as I kept on feeding them rabbit. Their presence seemed to keep the wild ones away. They bred fairly regularly, though not as quickly as the rabbits, but they only lived three or four years. I let them all go when I left.'

'Did you eat them?' I asked.

'Of course I ate them,' said the woman. 'I'd have starved otherwise.'

'Do you have any idea where they came from?' I asked.

'I thought they were something to do with the Project,' said the woman. 'That's what they looked like anyway. What do you think?'

She assumes that I know about the Project. Why should she assume that I know about the Project? Why don't I know about the Project?

'I never actually saw them,' I said. 'They used to come and scrape on the door early in the morning but they'd always gone by the time I'd got up.'

'They wanted you to feed them or pet them,' she said. 'I used to Sing to them. They seemed to enjoy that.'

'So what did they look like?' I asked.

The woman looked at me quizzically.

'You really never saw them, did you,' said the woman. 'You don't know anything about the Project either.'

'No I don't,' I said, plaintively. 'Please tell me.'

'It's not for me to tell you,' said the woman. 'Look, I'm tired now. I can't talk for long. It wears me out. Come another time.'

'Do you need anything?' I asked, getting up.

'No,' she said, lying back on the bed. 'There's nothing I need.'

I let myself out of the hut and walked through the village towards our house. Everything was very familiar. Everything was too familiar. Everything was not familiar at all.

As I neared our house, I grew increasingly fretful and apprehensive. In the dry Firth, I had sometimes thought about how I would greet our household upon my return. Now that I had returned, the fond scenes of reconciliation that I had rehearsed seemed shallow and contrived. I had walked away from Wave Singing. I had walked away from Goode. In our household everyone was answerable to everyone else but I still had more questions than answers.

I paused outside the front door of our house, wondering what to do. Perhaps it would be better to start by taking the manual to the Colony. Maybe the girl with the red hair and large feet would be pleased to see me after all. Perhaps I could spend the night there and come back here the next morning.

I was turning to leave when the door opened and my mother appeared, a worried look on her face. When she saw me, she stood on the hearth and smiled.

'It's you!' she said, quietly. 'I thought I heard something outside. I'm so glad to see you. Do come in.'

I followed my mother into the house. In the eating room, my father was sitting at the table in his best wheelchair.

'See who's here!' called my mother.

My father looked up at me and burst into tears.

'You're back!' cried my father. 'I knew you'd be back! Are you all right? We've all been so worried about you! You look well. A bit thin though. Haven't you been eating enough? Where have you been? We've all missed you so much! What did you find?'

'Let the lad alone,' said my mother, wiping the tears from his face with a large red-spotted handkerchief.

'Are you staying?' said my father.

'If I may,' I said.

'Don't be daft!' said my mother. 'Are you hungry?'

'I am,' I said, taking my bag off my back and sitting down at the table. 'I am.'

'Then I'll make you something,' said my mother, getting up.

This was a rare event. Not that my mother was a bad cook. But when she was writing she was often beset by demanding new notions, so her meals tended to be congealed or grey or burnt. Once, an unattended pressure cooker exploded, showering the kitchen with mashed potato. Since then my father did most of the cooking.

'I'll come and help you,' said my father.

My father wheeled himself across the eating room and down the corridor. I had forgotten how dignified and how open he was, his gentleness and generosity. Then I remembered how much these characteristics used to irritate and embarrass me and realised now how much they humbled me.

I looked round the eating room. Nothing had changed. It was as if I'd never left. Everything was where it had always been. But I had left.

Enticing smells wafted from the kitchen. My father trundled back into the eating room bearing a tray and parked himself next to me. On the tray was a large onion and spinach omelette and a stack of tortillas. The tortillas were fresh and the omelette was pungent with herbs. My mouth began to water. My mother set the tray on the table and sat down opposite me.

'Have you all eaten?' I asked, desperately hungry.

'We have,' said my mother. 'Help yourself.'

I cut myself a large wedge of omelette, which I wrapped in a tortilla and ate methodically. When I'd finished the wrap, I made and ate a second. All the while, my mother and father watched me patiently.

I finished the second wrap and sank back in the chair.

'Thank you,' I said to my mother.

'You're welcome,' she replied. 'Would you like anything else?'

'I'm really thirsty,' I said. 'I wouldn't mind something hot to drink.'

'The kettle's on,' said my mother, 'but we're running a bit low on chicory. How about some thyme?'

My mother knew I loathed thyme.

'How about some of this?' I said, reaching in my sack and passing her the bag of dried plants.

My mother inspected the bag.

'Oh!' said my mother, her eyes lighting up. 'That does look rather nice.'

'What have you got there?' asked my father, suspiciously.

'Nothing you'd like,' said my mother.

She quickly got up and took the bag from me.

'I'll not be long,' she said, and disappeared into the kitchen.

'It's so good that you're back,' said my father. 'I do hope you'll stay. We could do with a hand with the planting.'

'Where are the others?' I asked.

'Your older sister's up by the North Gate,' said my father. 'She met a nice young man on Kropotkin's Birthday and she's gone to stay with him.'

'So where are the twins?' I asked.

'They're in Town with Rufus and Goode,' said my father. 'They're due back on the barge tomorrow.'

'How is Goode?' I asked warily.

'She and the boy are thriving,' said my father. 'He looks just like you. You should go and see them once you've settled in.'

So I really was someone's father. I certainly didn't feel like someone's father. I hadn't ever thought about Goode bearing an actual child.

Stella

Nobody really wants me here. I just remind them of how bad things can get. Look at me, living like an animal amongst all their rubbish. Maybe I shouldn't have bothered coming back.

It'd be nice if Lucy came to see me again. She hates me calling her that. She says she's no time for names so that wee girl of hers still doesn't have one. She claims she's waiting to talk about it with the father. She won't tell me who he is though, not that I care. And she never mentions her sister. I might as well stop asking her things. At least she's strong and confident, not weak like me.

I can't help fingering the 'T' on my forehead. Every time I feel it, I ask myself why I couldn't have just let things be. Everyone knew where the food was and how much was left. And we'd all agreed the rations: nothing for the chronically ill, then more if you were older or younger. But I wasn't older or younger, and I couldn't bear it any longer: I was so hungry that I hurt all over. That's no excuse. Of course I stole for myself. But it wasn't just for me: I would have shared it with my daughters.

It was that calculating bitch Grace that called me out. She's never liked me. She stole Andrew from me but that wasn't enough for her. She just watched for her opportunity and, like the bloody fool I am, I gave it to her.

Who gave her the right to judge me? What made her so special? Of course her baby died. I'd never wished that on anyone, no matter how much I hated them. But lots of other peoples' babies died as well. At least she's got four more. I stole so I wouldn't lose mine; I lost them anyway.

After all this time she's not changed. She fixed me up and now I'm only here on her say so. I suppose I should be grateful: I know what I did was unforgivable.

It's cold now and there's not much left to eat. I hope Andrew comes soon. He usually brings me something tasty. He's good to me. He was always so forgiving.

Andrew's changed though. Look at him now, crippled by her arrogant bastard of a brother and full of all that Arkist bullshit.

The Arkists say that if we want to find freedom we have to accept suffering. My suffering's made a slave of me, no matter how much I deserved it. I wonder where that bloody Book of theirs came from. Someone must have written it. Did they know what it would do to people?

Andrew's so worried about his eldest boy. The lad never really said why he had to leave. At least he chose to go. At least he could choose.

I wasn't scared of the pain of the branding. I knew I deserved what was coming to me. And when they tore off my clothes I was too far gone to feel any shame. But I was terrified of trying to manage completely on my own. All my life I'd lived with other people.

After they forced me out into the waste land, they turned their backs on me and walked away. Everyone except Andrew. He waited until they'd gone and tossed me a bag over the fence. In it were a pair of old boots, a worn blanket, a skin of water and some hardtack. I'd never have made it without him. I wonder if the bitch knows he helped me.

It felt impossibly hard starting with nothing. I often thought I'd go mad without any other human company. Sometimes I wished they'd killed me. I couldn't ever kill myself though.

I got used to it. I made a life for myself. If I hadn't got so ill I suppose I'd still be there. But I couldn't face dying all alone. Even mouldering in this dung heap's better than that.

One winter I found a naked man lying unconscious by the burn. He was so thin that at first I hardly recognised him. He was from The Town but I'd never known him very well. He was a real mess. He'd an angry red 'R' burnt deep into his forehead, his feet were cut to ribbons and his groin was a putrid sore where they'd gelded him.

I felt nothing but loathing for him. He deserved to be thrown out far more than I did: I'd stolen food not innocence. But I could still show him some compassion even if no one had shown it to me.

I dragged him across to the hut on the sledge. Then I laid him by the fire, washed him and dressed his wounds. He seemed barely alive. I sat and looked at him, wondering what would happen if he revived.

Would he want to stay? If he did I'd not be lonely any more. And so much more could be done by two people. But would I want him to stay? Could I ever trust him? Who had he attacked? How could he do that to anyone?

He never came round and was dead by morning. I buried his poor wasted body under the potato patch, deep down so the beasts wouldn't find him.

I won't say his name. The Arkists think that naming things gives you power over them. Maybe that's why Lucy won't name her baby.

But that's all crap anyway. Naming things gives them power over you. Names don't just stand for things but for all of your history with them. They seem to sit there in the back of your head until you've almost forgotten them. Then when you're least expecting it they suddenly pop out and you remember lots of other stuff you'd rather not think about.

I never gave the beasts names. I suppose I grew too fond of them. Killing them was always hard. It was as if they knew what was coming to them, screaming and clawing as I moved in to finish them off. There was good meat on them, though, and their skins kept out the cold.

Everything's changed since I went away. There's so much I still don't properly understand. I'd really like to know how my girls wound up living in the Colony. Lucy won't tell me anything. I hope Andrew comes back soon. I must remember to ask him.

I can't have long to go now. The sores won't stop weeping and they're spreading.

Where will they bury me? Will they name a field for me?

I'm so cold. And I'm always so hungry. This is a lousy way to live and die.

16 My mother returned, carrying the steaming teapot and two mugs. She filled the mugs from the teapot, gave one to me and began to sip at the other.

'Aren't I having any?' asked my father plaintively.

'You wouldn't enjoy it,' said my mother firmly. 'You know it makes you querulous. Besides, you think it's for medicinal purposes.'

My father said nothing. It was clear that I had roused some long dormant disagreement.

'Have a wee dram,' said my mother, relenting. 'There's a fair bit left in the bottle she brought.'

'Who brought?' I asked.

'The red-headed girl from the Colony,' said my mother.

'Does she visit you?' I asked, surprised.

'She sometimes drops by when she goes to the market,' said my father.

'Does she come by herself?' I asked.

'She's always with the same young man,' said my father mysteriously. 'Your sister says he's the one who helped you when you broke your leg. We assumed they were together.'

So it had all been pointless. There was no hope for me. I felt completely washed out.

'We still don't know her name,' said my father.

'Nor do I,' I said bitterly.

My father raised his eyebrows. My mother shrugged . Then she fetched the bottle and a third mug from the kitchen and poured my father a generous slug of moonshine.

'*Slainte mhath*!' said my father, raising his mug.

'*Slainte mhor!*' chorused my mother and I in response.

We sat for a while, sipping quietly. I was exhausted and lost for words. My mother, her face aglow with relief, watched me expectantly. My father became increasingly restless, fidgeting with his mug until he spilt his whisky. My mother smiled and passed him the red spotted handkerchief. As he mopped at his knees, my father could stand it no more.

'Tell us all about it!' he urged me. 'Tell us everything!'

For the second time that evening, I recounted my journey to and from the dry Firth. Unlike the woman with the brand on her forehead, my parents listened intently and questioned me closely. They were particularly interested in the communications centre on top of the hill. I showed them the X-FLR6 manual. My mother carefully inspected the manual.

'Maybe this is it!' said my mother to my father, with an unfamiliar air of hope in her voice. 'Maybe this is it!'

'What do you mean?' I asked my mother. 'Is this something to do with the Project?'

My mother looked at my father. My father looked at my mother.

'You better take this to Rufus as soon as you can,' said my mother, handing the manual back to me. 'You could go on the barge tomorrow.'

'But he's only just back!' said my father. 'Shouldn't he stay for a bit?'

'This is much more important,' said my mother firmly. 'You know that.'

'Why won't you tell me about the Project?' I asked, feeling increasingly overwrought. 'Why won't you tell me after all I've been through?'

'You must have some idea about the Project,' said my mother, becoming uncharacteristically flustered. 'You've had long enough to think about it.'

'You know I don't!' I shouted. 'Just tell me!'

'No!' said my father. 'Not now. Not like this.'

'Why not now?' I shouted. 'Why is it never the right time? What are you hiding from me?'

'Just be a wee bit more patient,' said my mother. 'What you've found changes everything.'

'What's changed?' I shouted. 'Tell me what's changed!'

'You must be worn out,' said my father, rather too quickly. 'Why don't you move back into your old room. I'm sure the twins won't mind sharing now you're here again.'

'What do you mean 'move back in'?' I said, bewildered and deflected.

'Come on!' said my mother. 'You left and you didn't say if you were coming back. What were we supposed to do? We could hardly leave a room empty if someone else needed it.'

'But we've kept all your things,' said my father. 'Your siblings wanted to divide them up but we were sure you hadn't gone for good. They're all in the outhouse. You can get them in the morning'

'You can do what you like with my things!' I said. 'I want to know what I've got to do with this Project.'

'We can talk about it in the morning,' said my mother hastily. 'You should rest now. I'll tidy the room and make the bed for you.'

'Don't bother,' I said. 'Don't bother.'

I was very angry. I was very calm. I got up, picked up the backpack and went upstairs.

The room I used to sleep in was a guddle of clothes and possessions. I gathered everything in the centre of the bed, wrapped the bedding around it and dumped the bundle in the next door bedroom. Then I sat on the bed in the empty room.

I was too tired to think clearly. I was too tired to sleep. I could hear my parents arguing downstairs.

I swung the door to. Then I unpacked the backpack onto the table. My clothes were dirty and torn. The three arkles I'd made on my journey from the dry Firth were squashed and bent.

I took the remaining torn half page out of the back of the manual and folded it into an arkle. Then I placed the arkle on an open palm against my lips and sang to silence. The arkle didn't move. Again I sang beyond sound. The arkle fluttered briefly and fell still. I sat the arkle squarely on my flat palm and sang to it a third time. The arkle rose hesitantly from my hand and tumbled onto the floor.

As I bent over to retrieve the arkle, I saw a book under the bed. I reached under the bed and recovered the book. It was *The Green Child*. Goode must have left it behind. I put the book in the backpack. I could return the book to Goode when I went to the Town to see Rufus.

As I picked up the arkle, I noticed my mother standing quietly in the doorway watching me.

'I heard you from downstairs,' she said.

My mother came into the room and sat on the bed beside me.

'You really shouldn't damage books,' said my mother, taking the arkle from me.

Then she placed the arkle on her lap, took a deep breath and sang. The arkle rose vertically and stopped in mid-air in front of her face.

'Well,' said my mother, releasing the arkle from her voice. 'I didn't know that still worked.'

My mother passed the arkle back to me.

'Now it's your turn,' she said, playfully.

'Who taught you that?' I asked, my anger dissipated.

'I taught myself,' said my mother.

'How did you know it was possible?' I asked.

'The Wave Singer showed me,' said my mother, 'when he asked me to join them.'

I put the arkle on the bed between us.

'How did you hear me from downstairs?' I asked. 'I wasn't making any noise.'

'Yes you were,' said my mother. 'Not many people can hear it though.'

'Why not?' I asked.

'Why do you think?' said my mother.

'Is it something to do with the Project?' I asked.

'Yes,' said my mother.

'Are the Wave Singers part of the Project?' I asked.

'The Wave Singers are the main reason why the Project won't succeed,' said my mother, bitterly. 'The Wave Singers don't care about the Project. They want the Song for themselves, like addicts.'

'But they Sing for us all,' I said.

'They Sing for us all because that's all they're good for,' said my mother.

'Why should they be good at anything else? I asked. 'What difference does it make?'

'Think about who becomes Wave Singers,' said my mother. 'People who are good at Singing don't fit in anywhere else.'

'But their Singing holds us all together!' I said.

'Does it?' said my mother. 'Does it? Would we be any less united without Wave Singers?'

'But without the Wave Singers there's be no Singings,' I protested.

'Everyone learns to Sing,' said my mother. 'So why do we need Wave Singers? They're parasites. What else can they do apart from making arkles? They're only tolerated because everyone's forgotten why we have them in the first place.'

'How are they so different?' I asked.

'All they see is the Song,' said my mother. 'They're all corrupted by it. That's why I was so pleased when you didn't find your Stretch. I knew it wasn't too late for you.'

'But I did find my Stretch,' I said. 'And you found yours. But neither of us became Wave Singers.'

'That's the difference between Wave Singers and us,' said my mother. We care more about each other than about the Song.'

'But I thought you liked the Song,' I said, increasingly desperate

'Of course I like the Song!' said my mother. 'It's the most beautiful sound I've ever heard.'

'I really don't understand!' I said.

My mother looked directly at me and held her gaze in mine.

'You want to know about the Project,' she said. 'Well, we're the Project.'

'We're the Project?' I echoed, aghast.

'Yes,' said my mother. 'We're the Project .'

'Just us?' I asked, frightened.

'Just us,' said my mother. 'Just you and I.'

'No one else?' I persisted.

'No one else,' said my mother. 'Well, maybe Goode's child. But it's far too early to tell.'

'So that's why you and Rufus set me up!' I said.

'You set yourself up,' said my mother.

'Does Goode know we're the Project?' I asked.

'Of course she doesn't,' said my mother. 'I told you that before.'

'So who else knows?' I asked.

'The Project isn't a secret,' said my mother enigmatically. 'Everyone could know if they knew where to look. But people stopped caring years ago. Apart from our family.'

'Our family?' I said, puzzled. 'But there haven't been any families since the Event. Only households.'

'Don't be silly,' said my mother. 'Of course there are still families. The Event didn't change our biology. We still have DNA. We still inherit our parents' genes so we still inherit our parents' predispositions. Now go to bed.'

My mother got up and went downstairs, closing the door behind her.

I picked up the arkle and put it on my lap. Then I focused my whole being on the arkle and sang at it long and hard and silent. The arkle flew up to my face and then shot away across the bedroom.

I undressed and got into the sleeping bag. Shutting my eyes and my thoughts, I fell soundly asleep.

17 When I woke the next day, the sun was high. I dressed and went downstairs. My father was pottering in the kitchen.

'You slept a long time,' said my father. 'You must have been exhausted. Do you fancy some breakfast?'

'Yes please,' I said.

'Your mother's gone to work,' said my father. 'She says you're welcome to join her at the Fort. She's got a lot to tell you.'

'Why can't you tell me?' I asked him.

'It's better coming from her,' said my father. 'Why don't you go and shower. I'll make us both something to eat.'

'When's the barge due in?' I asked.

'Midday,' said my father. 'I thought I'd go and meet the twins.'

'I'll come with you,' I said.

I took a hurried shower and shared a plate of waffles with my father. Then I shouldered the backpack and we set off along the boardwalk to the Village basin. At the jetty there was a small crowd of people, chatting amiably as they watched for the barge to clear the lock and enter the canal that led to the basin. I wandered through the crowd, trying to spot the girl with the red hair, but I saw no one from the Colony.

I was returning to my father when I was hailed by our choir teacher.

'So you're back,' he said warmly, putting an arm around me. 'I hope you'll start coming to choir practice again. You've been hard to replace. No one else can hold the Stretches together in quite the same way.'

Our choir teacher's enthusiasm made me uneasy. My mother's

unexpected bile suggested that Singing might be more of a trap than a release.

'I don't think I'd be any use to the choir,' I said. 'I've not done much Singing for ages.'

'You picked it up again quickly enough before,' said our choir teacher. 'And it's not so long to the Autumn Singing. We've a good chance of winning this time.'

My father called from the end of the jetty. There was a brisk wind from the Glen and the barge was making good progress.

'I need to go to the Town,' I said, disengaging myself from our choir teacher. 'I'm not quite sure for how long.'

'Suit yourself,' said our choir teacher. 'But I hope you'll change your mind. I once found my Stretch, you know. Not quite as publicly as you though!'

As he turned away, he winked at me.

I felt a dull, nagging leaden-ness growing deep inside. Everybody knows. Everybody knows but me.

The barge came in close to the jetty. The barge master hailed me and threw me a rope. I looped the rope round the nearest bollard and hauled it tight. The barge master stepped ashore and took the rope from me.

'How's our Singer?' said the barge master, tying the rope to a stanchion on the deck.

'Have you got space for me?' I asked, as I helped her lay the gang plank.

'We could use another pair of arms to get us up to the lock,' said the barge master. 'But we're leaving straight away.'

The twins ran down the gang plank and hugged me. I stood there woodenly, lost in their warmth.

'Welcome back!' said my father, joining us. 'How was your visit? Here, give me your bags. How are Rufus and Goode?'

'We didn't see much of Rufus,' said a twin.

'Goode says he spends all his time just sitting in his office,' said the other twin.

'Goode's really worried about him,' said first twin.

'When she's not worrying about the baby,' said the other twin.

'Who looks just like you,' said the first twin.

'That's enough!' said my father. 'Let's go home now.'

The twins raced off along the jetty.

'Aren't you coming?' said my father to me.

'No,' I said. 'I need to go to the Town.'

'Yes,' said my father. 'Yes. I know that. We'll be seeing you then.'

He unbraked the wheelchair and set off behind the twins.

The barge master blew her whistle. I went up the gang plank and joined the bargees and the other passengers on the low cross benches. The barge master hauled up the gang plank, cast off, took the tiller seat in the stern and began to chant. We picked up the oars and began to row in time to the chanting.

As we entered the lock the wind swung round behind the barge. As we left the lock, the bargees raised the sail. As we traversed the Loch, I sat in the prow but this time I didn't Sing. As the sun went down, I unrolled my sleeping bag under the awning and went to sleep.

It was early next morning when the barge docked at the Town quay. I helped unload the barge. Then I walked across the Town to my uncle's house.

My father told me nothing. I didn't want to see Goode. My mother told me riddles. I didn't want to see the child. What might Rufus tell me?

I stopped outside the house. Inside, a baby was crying. I knocked on the front door. After a long pause, Goode opened the door, a mewling babe in her arms.

'So it's you,' she said, emotionless. 'Come in and meet your son.'

'Is Rufus here?' I asked, following her into the hall.

'What's become of you?' she asked, sharply. 'Don't you have any time for us?'

'Of course I've time for you,' I said, awkwardly, 'but I really need to see Rufus.'

'I thought I'd never see you again,' she said. 'Did you ever think of me?'

'Of course I thought of you,' I said, too earnestly.

'Did you find whatever you were looking for?' asked Goode.

'I don't know what I was looking for,' I said, 'and I don't know what I've found. I don't even know what I am any more. I'm sick of evasions and half truths. That's why I need to talk to Rufus.'

'You're making no sense' said Goode, exasperated. 'Dad's at work. But you'll not get much sense out of him either.'

'What's happened to Rufus?' I asked, concerned.

'You'll see,' said Goode. 'Off you go.'

'I'll be back later,' I said.

'We're not going anywhere,' said Goode.

I should have looked for Rufus when I arrived.

I walked back to the quay, into the Store and went down into the cellars to Rufus' office.

The office door was open. Rufus was sitting at his desk, bent over a brass microscope. He paid no attention when I came in. I went over and stood opposite him.

'What are you doing?' I asked.

'Have a look,' said Rufus, sliding the microscope across the desk towards me.

There was a shiny disk clamped onto the microscope platform. The disc looked like the one we had listened to on my last visit. I peered down through the eyepiece and tried to focus.

'I don't know what I'm looking at,' I said.
'Let me,' said Rufus.

He came round to my side of the desk and adjusted the microscope.

'What do you see now?' asked Rufus. .
'Lots of bubbles,' I said. 'Should they be there?'
'Of course they shouldn't!' said Rufus.
'What causes them?' I asked.
'Age,' said Rufus. 'The discs are finally wearing out.'
'How long are they supposed to last?' I asked.
'Hundreds of years,' said Rufus.

Hundreds of years. So it has been hundreds of years since the Event.

'Aren't there paper copies?' I asked, foolishly.
'Do you have any idea how much information one of these holds?' said Rufus. 'Of course there aren't paper copies!'
'How many discs are there,' I asked.

Rufus got up, crossed the room and opened a double-door, ceiling-high metal cabinet. The metal cabinet was completely full of discs in their cases.

'These are just a fraction of the records we have from before the Event,' said Rufus. 'The rest are in the Fort. What are we going to do when they've gone?'

'They're not much use now if we can't read them,' I said, sardonically.

'But we might still be able to read them!' said Rufus. 'If only we could restart the Bootstrapping. But no one will listen to me. They all say we've tried once and it failed so there's no point in trying again.'

'The Colonists don't think that,' I said.

'The Colonists are dreamers,' said Rufus. 'They want to stay here and rebuild everything from scratch. I want to leave.'

'But there's nowhere to go,' I said.

'Of course there is!' said Rufus. 'If only we could talk to the satellite.'

'Might this help?' I asked, removing the X-FLR6 manual from the backpack and passing it to him.

Rufus took the manual from me, looked at the cover and started to laugh.

'What's so funny,' I asked, offended. 'I spent half a year getting it back.'

'Well you wasted your time,' said Rufus.

'Why won't it help?' I asked bewildered.

'It isn't just the discs,' said Rufus. 'Everything's slowly decaying. Electronic components are becoming more and more faulty. We've no spares for most of them and there's no way to patch up integrated circuits. We've no reliable source of energy so we can't even test the communication equipment we have left. How can we possibly talk to the satellite?'

'The Colonists think they can,' I said stubbornly.

Rufus snorted at me.

'Look,' I said. 'I really came here to find out about the Project.'

'The Project doesn't matter anymore!' said Rufus, thrusting the manual at me. 'Now you're wasting my time. I've work to do. Just go away.'

Astonished and upset, I took the manual and left the Store.

Across the quay where the barge was moored, I asked the bargees when they were returning to the Village. The barge master said that they were waiting for supplies. The barge wouldn't leave until the following morning.

I walked back to the house and let myself in. Goode was sitting by the fire. The baby was asleep on her lap. Goode barely glanced up at me.

I sat down on the bench and began to cry. Goode laid the baby in the basket at her feet and took me in her arms.

'Not you as well,' said Goode. 'Not you as well.'

18

We sat huddled together until I had stopped shaking. Then Goode gently released me.

'Will you be alright now?' she asked me.

'Thank you,' I said, unconvincingly. 'I'll be fine.'

Goode got up and went back to her chair.

'Dad should be home for lunch soon,' she said. 'Will you eat with us before you go?'

'The barge doesn't leave until tomorrow,' I said. 'I was hoping I could stay here.'

'You know you're welcome,' said Goode, politely.

It was clear that I was anything but welcome. I said nothing.

The baby woke and started to bleat. Goode lifted the baby out of the basket.

'Here,' said Goode, passing me the baby. 'You take him. I'll make lunch.'

'What's he called?' I asked.

'I thought you'd never ask!' said Goode. 'I haven't named him yet. I waited for you.'

'You should name him,' I said.

I cautiously sat the baby on my knee. The baby's cries grew louder. I gently bounced the baby up and down. The baby stopped crying and smiled at me. When the baby smiled he looked like my mother. My parents said that when I was young I looked like my mother. I offered the baby my right pinkie. The baby grasped my finger and began to suck it.

'I think he's hungry,' I said to Goode, who was rolling out tortillas on the table.

'He can't be hungry,' said Goode. 'I fed him just before you came in.'

The baby grew restless and began to whimper. I tried bouncing the baby up and down again but he grew louder. I stood up and put the baby over my left shoulder. Then I walked round and round the table, Singing to the baby. The baby grew calmer and fell asleep.

'He seems to like my Singing,' I said to Goode.

'You still Sing beautifully,' said Goode, 'but I really don't think he cares.'

'Why not?' I asked, chagrined.

'Because he can't hear you,' said Goode. 'He's deaf.'

'He's deaf?' I said, aghast. 'Will he be able to Sing?'

'I don't even know if he'll be able to talk,' said Goode. 'I'm going to teach him to sign when he's older.'

I carefully laid the baby down in the basket.

'I'm so sorry, ' I said.

'Don't be,' said Goode. 'He's a braw wee boy. What else could I ask for?'

She turned back to the tortillas.

'What's happened to Rufus?' I asked. 'He's never been so short with me before.'

'These days he's short with everyone,' said Goode. 'Even Gaye. He says no one listens to him any longer. He says he feels isolated and ineffective. But he shouldn't take it out on us. He's just making things worse.'

'When did it start?' I asked.

'He was really excited when I told him I was pregnant,' said Goode. 'He kept talking about how hopeful it made him for the future. When we found out that the bairn was deaf he seemed to slump right back inside himself, they way he was after mum died.'

'Do you have any idea why?' I asked.

'He's always been really fond of Singing,' said Goode. 'We all knew he was disappointed that none of us could Sing. I'm best of the four of us and I can barely hold a Stretch. Anyway, all through my pregnancy he kept saying how important it was for the bairn to be a Singer. When you were chosen at the Autumn Singing he was elated, as if it was a sign that the bairn would Sing like you.'

'Did he ever say why it mattered so much to him?' I asked.

'It never came up,' said Goode. 'Mum was a good Singer though. Maybe he wanted some sort of renewal of a part of her he'd loved most.'

I took the eighth of the torn page out of the back of the X-FLR6 manual and folded it into an arkle.

'I wonder if we could teach the boy to do this,' I said.

'I'm sure he'll learn how to make arkles,' said Goode, scathingly.

'Just wait,' I said, placing the arkle on the table and singing to it.

The arkle rose from the table.

'How did you do that?' asked Goode, amazed. 'I've never seen anyone do that before.'

'Can't Rufus do it?' I asked.

'If he can he's never shown us,' said Goode.

'Well I can do it and so can my mother,' I said. 'So can the oldest Wave Singer.'

'It's just a trick, isn't it,' said Goode.

'I think it's more than a trick,' I said. 'I think it's to do with the Project.'

'I thought the Project was a way for us all to escape from here,' said Goode.

Tell her. Tell her.

'My mother claims that she and I are the Project,' I said, slowly.

'What are you saying?' said Goode, plainly shocked. 'How can individuals be a Project?'

'I don't really know,' I said. 'She said no one else is except maybe your boy.'

'Our boy,' said Goode.

'Our boy,' I acknowledged. 'She hinted that it's something to do with being a very good Singer but not becoming a Wave Singer.'

'What's the point of being a good Singer if it isn't your life?' asked Goode.

'I didn't understand until I had to choose,' I said.

'What's the Project got to do with us?' asked Goode.

'I don't really know,' I said, 'but I'm pretty sure it's why my mother and Rufus were so keen for us to get together.'

'That's crazy!' said Goode, agitatedly. 'I was keen for us to get together! It was nothing to do with them! I wanted it!'

Perhaps Goode really did know nothing of the Project. Perhaps Goode really did choose me. That made me feel even worse.

Rufus came through the front door. He stopped short when he saw the arkle.

'What's that doing here?' he asked gruffly.

I quickly sang at the arkle. The arkle rose up and floated across the table to Rufus. Rufus sat down and looked at me strangely.

'Just like Sally,' he said quietly.

'I never knew mum could do that,' said Goode, indignantly.

'You do now,' said Rufus.

'Why didn't she ever show us?' asked Goode.

'My mother never showed us either,' I said.

'No,' said Rufus. 'She wouldn't. What did she tell you about the Project.'

'Not much,' I said. 'She thinks she's protecting me.'

'She was always soft when it came to family,' said Rufus.

'But we don't have families anymore!' exclaimed Goode. 'Just households.'

'Mother, father, brother, sister, uncle, aunt, nephew, niece, cousin,' said Rufus. 'Why do we still need all these words if we don't have families anymore?'

'They're the people we grow up with and the people they grew up with,' said Goode. 'They don't mean anything else. You've no biological connection to his father,' nodding at me. 'He's got no biological connection to mum.'

'We're all connected,' said Rufus.

'Hundreds of thousands of years ago, maybe,' I said.

'Much more recently than that,' said Rufus darkly. 'How many people do you think survived the Event?'

'Several thousand,' said Goode. 'How else would our community have been viable?'

'Far too many,' said Rufus.

'Several hundred?' I asked.

'Far too many,' said Rufus.

'So how many then?' asked Goode.

'At least two,' said Rufus. 'For starters.'

'But we'd all be badly inbred,' I protested. 'Lots of us would have inherited diseases like haemophilia.'

'Not if there's enough genetic mutation,' said Rufus. 'Anyway, why do you think we aren't all badly inbred? Why do you think there are so many twins? Where do you think Wave Singing comes from?'

'What are you saying?' asked Goode. 'Surely we're not just some breeding programme!'

'That's exactly what we are,' said Rufus.

'Just how long ago was the Event?' I asked.

'Now that's a good question,' said Rufus.

'You must have some idea,' I said.

'Work it out for yourself,' said Rufus airily. 'How many people are there now?'

'Around five thousand,' said Goode.

'How many generations is that starting from two people?' asked Rufus.

I thought for a minute.

'Eleven or twelve,' I said, 'with simple doubling every generation.'

'So how long at forty years for each generation?' asked Rufus.

'Going on five hundred years?' said Goode.

'Five hundred years?' I echoed. 'That can't be right.'

'Well,' said Rufus, 'it's probably an underestimate.'

'How's that possible?' said Goode. 'How could all the things we use have lasted for so long?'

'That's another good question,' said Rufus. 'None of us know. What do you think?'

'I thought there were records,' I said.

'There are,' said Rufus, 'but they only go back a couple of hundred years.'

'What do they say?' asked Goode.

'They make grim reading,' said Rufus. 'Ask my sister to show you.'

'There's no need,' I said.

I told them of the deserted settlement and of the underground room full of bones. Rufus sat awkwardly, not looking at me, picking at his cuticles. Goode, spellbound, watched me closely.

'Well,' said Rufus when I'd finished. 'You've had a hard time of it. And all for nothing. Still, now you know almost as much as any of us.'

'Almost as much?' I said. 'What else is there?'

'Not much more,' said Rufus, obliquely.

'Why not just tell us everything?' said Goode. 'Why shouldn't we know?'

'What would be the point?' said Rufus. 'What difference would it make now?'

'You said you'd always tell us the truth,' said Goode. 'You said we should know where we came from and where we're going.'

'You want the truth?' said Rufus. 'Well, the truth is that everything's crumbled away. The Bootstrapping failed. His father's a cripple. Sally's dead. The Project's broken…'

'I really can't take any more of your self pity,' said Goode.

She picked up the baby and went outside. I turned to Rufus. Rufus shrugged at me. I picked up my bag and followed Goode into the garden.

'I can't stand it when he gets like this,' said Goode, sitting down on the wooden bench next to the front door.

'Does it happen a lot?' I asked.

'More and more,' said Goode.

'What are you going to do?' I asked.

'There's not much I can do,' said Goode.

'You could come back to the Village,' I said.

'And live with you?' said Goode. 'I don't think so, do you?'

I said nothing.

'Right,' said Goode. 'No surprises there then. So what are you going to do now?'

'I'll be on my way,' I said.

'But you said the boat wasn't going today,' said Goode.

'I'll walk,' I said. 'It'll only take a couple of days. Maybe I can pick up the barge along the lochside.'

'You really are welcome to stay,' said Goode.

'I know that,' I said. 'But I think it's best if I go.'

'We haven't named the boy,' said Goode. 'You can't leave 'til we've named him.'

I thought for a while.

'We could call him Salvador,' I said, finally. 'For your mum.'

'Salvador,' said Goode. 'The saviour. I wonder who he'll save.'

I reached into the bag and found *The Green Child*.

'You left this behind,' I said.

'Keep it,' said Goode. 'Bring it back next time you're passing.'

'I'll be off then,' I said, returning the book to the bag.

'Goodbye,' said Goode. 'Take care of yourself.'

'*Sauve qui peut*,' I said. 'Goodbye.'

Along the road I looked back but Goode and Salvador had gone.

I was sad to leave. I was glad to leave.

The Book of Loss

. . .

contraband

contraception

contracts

conventicles

conventions

convicts

convictions

convocations

co-ownership

cor blimey trousers

cordless phones

corduroy

coriander

corgis

cork

cormorants

corn dogs

corneal grafts

corned beef

cornets

cornflakes

corn plasters

coronets

coronations

corporations

correspondence courses

corrugated cardboard

corsets

corticosteroids

cosmetic surgery

cosmonauts

cost cutting

cottleston pie

cotton

council tax

councillors

counsellors

courts

covenants

covert operations

cows

coypu

. . .

All Around

19 I walked through the Town to the Store. The Diner was open so I went in and straight over to the servery where I helped myself to a bowl of soup and a hunk of corn bread. I looked around but I didn't see anyone that I knew. Sitting down at one end of the long table by the window, I began to eat the soup.

I ate without looking up. I was very hungry. I was always very hungry these days.

I was wiping round the bowl with the last piece of bread when Blythe entered the Diner. She spotted me, and came over and stood beside me.

'I'd heard you were in town,' she said. 'You weren't at home so I wondered if I'd find you in the Store.'

'Well here I am,' I said.

'Can I join you?' asked Blythe.

'Of course,' I said.

She went round the table and sat down opposite me.

'Aren't you eating?' I asked.

'Maybe later,' said Blythe. 'Are you sticking around for a while?'

'No,' I said. 'I'm going back to the Village.'

'That's probably the best thing to do,' said Blythe. 'Things have been really crap since Goode had the baby. Dad's gone crazy, the way he was after mum died, and Goode's even more martyred, if that's possible.'

'How's Gaye?' I asked. 'I haven't seen her this time.'

'Gaye's fine,' said Blythe. 'How are you?'

'Tired and weary,' I said. 'I'm surprised you're interested.'

'Wired and teary,' said Blythe. 'Why shouldn't I be interested.'

'You've never had much time for me before,' I said.

'I thought you were a wee prick,' said Blythe, 'but leaving like that was just great.'

'I just ran away,' I said.

'Who cares?' said Blythe. 'You really screwed up their plans.'

'What plans?' I asked.

I knew the answer.

'The Project of course,' said Blythe.

'How do you know about the Project?' I asked.

'It was all they ever talked about,' said Blythe. 'Mum and dad, and your parents. Not in front of the children, of course, but you'd have to be as dim as Goode not to see what was going on. You're well out of it.'

'Well out of what?' I persisted.

'Don't be so coy,' said Blythe. 'The boy won't be able to Sing, so Goode must have asked you to have another and you must have turned her down.'

'We never even discussed it,' I said.

'Really?' said Blythe, surprised. 'Really?'

'Really,' I said. 'Goode's besotted with Salvador even if Rufus isn't.'

'Salvador?' said Blythe.

'That's what we've called him,' I said. 'So why were you looking for me?'

'We're starting a new household,' said Blythe. 'On the other side of the basin.'

'What's so new about it?' I asked, conversationally.

'We're going to do things differently,' said Blythe, earnestly. 'No more Singing. No more Ark. No more duty. No more obligation.

We're going to make big changes.'

'Do you really think that'll work?' I asked, sceptically.

'It'll work if we can find the right people,' said Blythe. 'That's why I was trying to find you. I wanted to ask you to join us.'

'Who's 'us'?' I asked.

'Other people who think the same way,' said Blythe. 'People who are fed up with the way things are, who want to live in the present, not the past or the future.'

Was I one of those people? I was tired of the way things were but the past and the future both seemed better than the present.

'Thanks,' I said, 'but I've got to finish what I started.'

'As you like,' said Blythe. 'If you change your mind you'll know where to find us. I'll see you around then.'

Blythe got up and left the Diner.

What had I started? What did I have to finish?

I took my bowl through to the kitchen and added it to the pile in the deep enamelled sink.

'What's doing?' I asked the man at the stove.

'You could wash up,' said the man. 'Or you could start some more soup.'

'Is there any hot water?' I asked.

'I've only just put it on,' said the man.

'I'll chop the veg then,' I said. 'I need to be on my way fairly soon.'

'Do you know where things are?' asked the man. 'I've not seen you here before.'

'I've not been here for a while,' I said. 'But I'm sure I'll find everything.'

The kitchen was well-organised. Pans hung on hooks above the sink. The chopping board was next to a large wooden block of knives on the work surface beside the sink. The vegetables were stored on latticed racks in a deep cupboard on the back wall of the kitchen.

I spent the next hour peeling and paring and slicing and chopping and bantering with the man by the stove.

It was good to be busy with someone else, to share a simple common purpose. I thought Blythe so wrong to shun mutualism. If you work you eat. If you eat you work. Everyone knows that. What else is there?

When I'd filled a large copper pan with finely chopped shallots and fennel and swede and curly kale, I washed down the board and knife and put them by the sink to dry.

'I'll be off now,' I said to the man by the stove.
'Do you need anything for your journey?' he asked me.
'Could you spare some bread?' I asked him.
'Sure,' said the man by the stove. 'Help yourself.'

I put a loaf of corn bread into the bag and left the Diner. From the Store, I took the road through the park towards the quay.

On the bandstand in the park, the gamelan orchestra were practising. I stood for a while and listened to the echoing chimes of the gongs and metallophones. In gamelan, like Singing, the voices play with and against and across each other. But gamelan has an austere and predictable quality, where the Song is warm and plastic, constantly changing like the waves on the shore. The Colonists would build machines to play gamelan. I wondered if the girl with red hair and large feet preferred gamelan to Singing. The girl with red hair had the makings of a fine Singer.

I left the park and followed the road past the quay and out of town. Beyond the basin, at the start of the chain of locks, I turned off the road onto the gravel towpath. The path left the town behind and wound its way up the hill beside the vast stone locks. I had last walked this way with my mother, so long ago. At the highest lock, the towpath levelled out and traced the Loch shore through the Glen.

As I walked, there was a steady breeze at my back. There would be no call to row the barge on a day like this. The wind drove white-crested waves across the water to break rhythmically on the shore. I stopped and shut my eyes and listened to the waves and the shore Singing their Stretch of the Loch.

I opened my eyes and resumed my journey but as I walked, the Loch's Song called to me. Despite our teacher's admonitions, we had always treated the old recordings from the Fort as our Song's ideal. How might I Sing with a living Stretch which changed with every breath of the breeze?

Then I remembered the rounds we'd sung as children, where each singer repeated the phrase the previous singer had just completed. Perhaps I could Sing each breaking wave back to the Loch.

I left the path and went down the gentle slope to the shore where the waves broke onto a long, thin, sandy beach. I took off my shoes and socks and put them in my bag. Then I walked slowly along the beach, the soft fine sand blowing across my toes, watching and listening to the waves. As each wave broke, I tried to gather its breaking with my breath and reflect it back across the Loch.

At first it was hard to keep up with the Loch. There seemed to be no pattern; I had to concentrate hard to Sing each breaking wave in just enough time to catch the next. After a while, I began to sense how the sound of each wave was shaped by the shore which shattered it. As I walked, I relaxed into the rhythm rather than the pattern of the waves. As I Sang each wave, I began to feel how the next wave would break on the shore ahead.

Late in the afternoon, I came to a small semicircular bay. I knelt by the water's edge and drank from my cupped hands. Then I sat back on the sand and listened to the Loch. The breeze and the waves had died away, and the water lapped at the shore of the bay.

I began to softly Sing the Song of the Loch which steadily blended with mine until we Sang as if with one voice. Then the breeze picked up and the waves began to build and the Loch's Song grew faster and louder and my Song grew stronger and more urgent and I had the sudden sensation of looking down, above the bay, above the Loch, above the Glen, above the Island, above the oceans, above the continents, above the small bluey-green ball circling the yellow sun, above the sea of stars, above endless black space.

I had been here before. Enwrapped in the nothingness, but calm and alert, perhaps I had found my Stretch once more. But across the hurtling depths of void, across the twisting folds of change, I could still hear the Loch's Song and I could still sense myself Singing by the Loch side. It wasn't my Stretch and I hadn't found it. The Loch's Stretch had found me.

I gently stopped Singing and eased back into myself and sat quietly in the sun, cross legged, as the waves broke on the shore around me.

Now I knew why the Wave Singers would never find their Stretches. The Songs of the Wave Singer were sad shadows of long dead Stretches. A Wave Singer was fortunate if they could meld their Song with a frozen Stretch just once in a lifetime. But the Loch's Stretch lived in the endless change of the wind and the waves and the shore. Perhaps anyone could be found by a living Stretch if they let it shape their Song.

I ate half of the corn bread and drank from the Loch. Then I put on my shoes and socks, shouldered the bag and set off down the towpath. I walked for a couple of hours but I didn't Sing. I felt replete with Song and was content to watch the water and listen to the Loch.

Early in the evening, I came to a jetty projecting out into the Loch. A path led from the landing stage into the woods. I took the path through the rustling gum trees. The shimmering smell of eucalyptus oils reminded me of my father's potions for aches and sprains.

The path broadened out into a wide clearing. Around the perimeter, small windmills on tall poles drove intricately articulated figures that folded in and out of tai chi poses. High above the centre of the clearing, a larger windmill propelled a set of deep chimes.

I stopped and listened as the chimes rang the changes on its wooden tubular bells. The measured repetition reminded me of the gamelan orchestra I had heard that morning. I walked up to the chimes and watched the cogs thrust the strikers against the bells. The rotating cogs reminded me of the clocks in the house in the Colony.

20 As the sun set, I crossed the clearing and followed the path deeper into the woods. The path led gently uphill towards a ridge where the woods ended. At the edge of the woods, I looked down across a narrow river valley backed by mountains. In the centre of the valley stood a squat, stout Ark surrounded by cottages. This Ark was quite unlike those in our Village and the Town. It was solidly built, from clinker-laid planks and looked as if it really could survive the Great Flood. Light shone from the Ark's open ramp and smoke rose from its funnel.

From the ridge, steep steps led down the incline to the valley floor. I went down the steps and across the valley. There was nobody about as I walked through the Settlement. As I approached the Ark, I began to hear low chanting. As I neared the Ark, the chanting grew louder.

I had heard this chanting before from the Village Ark; the Arkists were Placating the Flood. My father sometimes went to this weekly ceremony. He said he found it uplifting. When the Great Flood came, the chanting would sustain the Ark. When the Great Flood comes we'll need more than chanting, said my mother scathingly, paring his toe nails with the sewing scissors.

Placating the Flood, like all Arkist rituals, was open to everyone. From my father's rambling account, Placating the Flood sounded pointless and dull. When I reached the Ark, I decided to wait for the ritual to end before seeking shelter.

I sat down on the bench next to the ramp. To pass the time, I took the remaining quarter page from the X-FLR6 manual and folded it into an arkle. Then I placed the arkle on my palm in front of my face and Sang at it. As the arkle rose from my hand, the chanting stopped abruptly and the Arkists rushed from the Ark.

'They have come! They have come!' cried the Arkists, surrounding me.

The Arkistant, his long white robe stained with candle grease, knelt in front of me.

'You have come!' he said loudly, proffering me his staff of office.

I sat on the bench, profoundly shocked.

'You have come!' said the Arkistant again, still proffering his staff.

'But I don't understand!' I stuttered.

The Arkistant looked me in the eye and winked.

'Take the bloody thing,' said the Arkistant, *sotto voce*, 'bow to me, and get yourself into the Ark. Now!'

Uncertain what else to do, I stood up, took the staff from the Arkistant, bowed to him and walked up the ramp into the Ark. The Arkistant followed me, drawing the ramp shut behind us.

The Ark was walled and roofed with close-fitting boards that had once been painted white. The walls were studded with small candle holders in the shape of arkles. A lighted candle sat in the prow of each arkle. The wax from the guttering candles ran down the walls of the Ark onto the myriad of tiny arkles that covered the floor. In the prow of the Ark was a raised wooden dais surmounted by an enormous, intricately carved arkle, with a large burning candle in its prow.

The Arkistant took his staff from me and sat down on a chair in front of the dais.

'Have a seat! Have a seat!' he said, patting the chair next to him. 'I haven't had so much fun for ages! I saw you at the Autumn Singing but I'd never expected you to show up here!'

'What's happening?' I asked.

'Are you The One?' asked the Arkistant, beaming at me.

'The one what?' I said.

'The One who will Raise the Ark,' said the Arkistant, trying not to laugh.

'Don't be ridiculous!' I said. 'How could any one person raise this Ark?'

'Exactly!' said the Arkistant, taking the staff from me. 'We better go and tell them.'

The Arkistant got up, lowered the ramp and stood in the doorway of the Ark, holding his staff aloft. I stood behind him, anxious as to what would happen next.

'It is not They!' intoned the Arkistant, solemnly.

'It is not They!' chorused the Arkists, nonchalantly.

The Arkists began to disperse. The Arkistant turned to me.

'Sorry about that,' said the Arkistant. 'I can see you've got no idea what we're up to.'

'How did you know I was outside?' I asked.

I knew the answer.

'I heard you Singing, of course,' said the Arkistant. 'How else do you think I knew you were there?'

'Did anyone else hear me?' I asked.

'The other Wave Singers,' said the Arkistant. 'There are quite a few of us here.'

'What's all that about 'The One'?' I asked.

'For it is written,' said the Arkistant:

And One shall be Seated before you.
And their Song shall Raise the Ark.
And the Great Flood shall be Placated.
And those who are Raised with the Ark shall be
Made Whole by the Great Flood.

'Who wrote that?' I asked.

'Your mother, I expect,' said the Arkistant. 'She wrote most of our texts.'

'My mother?' I said, utterly astonished. 'How could she possibly have written them? Surely they're all far older than her.'

'The Ark's as old as Wave Singing,' said the Arkistant. 'But the rituals were passed by word of mouth and had become incoherent. Your mother was asked to clarify and unify them, that's all. She's a fine imagination and a good ear for incantation. Attendance really picked up once she'd finished.'

'But my mother's got no time for Arkism,' I said.

'She likes to tell a good story though,' said the Arkistant. 'Listen. Before the Event there was a really strange religion called Christianity. Christians worshiped a tortured god and their holy book, The Bible, was written in languages that only a small number of people could read. Anyway, sixteen hundred years after it was supposed to have been written, a king decided to give his subjects a translation that they could all understand, so he set up a committee to write a definitive version. Now, all the people on the committee were highly educated. Do you really think they all believed every last word that they wrote? Of course they didn't. But their translation has some of the most beautiful prose ever written. It's called The Authorised Version. Your mother's sure to have a copy somewhere. It's got one of the earliest accounts of the Great Flood.'

'But religion's obscene!' I said. 'How could my mother possibly promote it?'

'Your mother may be a pornographer,' said the Arkistant. 'but

Arkism isn't a religion. We don't worship through blind superstition. We celebrate meteorological certainty. And why shouldn't we use fine words and images in our celebration?'

'So what does 'Made Whole' mean?' I asked.

'I don't have a clue,' said the Arkistant. 'It does sound nice though.'

'So how do you know my mother?' I asked.

'I chose her,' said the Arkistant. 'I was so relieved when she turned me down. Her Song was lustrous but she'd have made a poor Wave Singer. She was far too wilful. Much like you. She's a splendid writer. She's far more use to us writing pornography.'

'More use to us?' I said, remembering my uncle's words. 'We don't use people!'

'Do you still believe that?' said the Arkistant. 'Of course we use people. Mutual aid is the ultimate manipulation. Maximum co-operation optimises individual outcomes. Everyone studies that at school. It's basic games theory.'

'But this isn't a game!' I insisted.

The Arkistant had lost interest and was closing the Ark.

'Let's be off,' said the Arkistant. 'You'll need somewhere to stay. There's a spare bed in the Ark House. Have you got a sleeping bag?'

The Arkistant set off round to the back of the Ark, leaning on his staff and humming to himself. I followed him pensively.

The Ark House was a single story octagonal building, on stilts to keep it above the Great Flood. The Arkistant clambered up the ladder to the veranda. I climbed up behind him. The Arkistant took off his shoes and entered the Ark House.

'This way,' he said.

The front door let into a large carpeted sitting room. In the sitting room, the Arkists sat in padded armchairs round the stone fireplace, whittling tiny arkles from blocks of ghost gum and tossing the shavings onto the fire. They looked up and smiled as we came into the sitting room but nobody said anything.

'There's a bed through here,' said the Arkistant, opening a door on the left of the sitting room and leading me into a spartan dormitory divided into six cubicles.

'This one's free,' said the Arkistant, pointing to a cubicle.

In the cubicle, on the bare floor, was a crude box bed lined with a worn sheep skin.

'Let's eat,' said the Arkistant.

The Arkistant led me back through the empty sitting room to the dining room. In the dining room, the Arkists stood silently round the rectangular table. The Arkistant went into the kitchen and returned with a trolley bearing a rack of lamb, a bucket of baked sweet potatoes and a jug of gravy. He helped himself from the trolley, pushed it round to the Arkist on his left, sat down and began to eat. I stood at the only empty space, on the Arkistant's right and watched as each Arkist served themselves and passed the trolley on. There was a generous helping of food left on the trolley when it finally reached me.

The Arkists ate quietly and systematically. As I ate, my brain raced.

If this was all a game, what sort of game was it? We played lots of different games at school and at home. Counting games and singing games. Word games and number games. Card games and board games. Co-operative games and competitive games. Games of planning. Games of chance. Games of deception.

Once, at school, we played a very old board game which

involved accumulating tokens of wealth and property at everybody else's expense. I found this game frustrating and tiresome. Our teacher said that it was supposed to show us how most people lived before the Event.

In the books my mother read, games were a common theme. Sometimes people sought personal gain or tried to escape unbearable lives through games. Sometimes they were forced to play games to amuse their masters or their enemies.

In my mother's science fiction stories, sometimes people accidentally discovered that they were unwitting players or pieces in a game, perhaps on an alien planet or in a table top world or inside a computer. But in our world there were no aliens or giants or computers.

If our life was a game, who were the players and what were the pieces? What were the rules and who made them? Who won and who lost? Our lives were starkly real. How could this be a game?

After supper, the Arkistant put his plate and cutlery onto the trolley, got up, pushed the trolley round to the Arkist on his left and left the dining room. When the trolley reached me, I was the last person in the dining room. I put my plate and cutlery and the remains of food onto the trolley and pushed it through to the kitchen.

21 The kitchen was empty. The sink was full of hot water. I found containers for the remains of the food, which I stood on a shelf in the larder. Then I unloaded the trolley into the sink and washed the dirty utensils.

I was scrubbing the last dish when I felt an uncanny purple sensation inside the back of my skull. I thought I must be tired. I shook my head but the sensation persisted and grew stronger. I put the platter onto the drying rack and went back into the dining room.

The Arkists were sitting round the dining table, broad smiles on their faces. In front of each Arkist, a tiny arkle hovered in the air. When he saw me, the Arkistant stopped Singing and caught his arkle in his right hand.

'Come and join us,' he said, passing me the arkle and taking another from a pocket in his robe.

I sat at the table next to the Arkistant. I managed to raise the arkle but I could not hold it aloft for long, so I sat quietly and watched the Arkists.

First they shuttled their arkles round and round the table from Singer to Singer. Then they began to juggle their arkles back and forth to each other across the table, adding more and more arkles until each Singer held half a dozen aloft. The flying arkles wove increasingly intricate patterns above the table, dancing from Singer to Singer. The Arkists occasionally dropped their arkles, and silently, with wry faces, mocked each other's lack of skill.

Finally, to mark the end of the evening, the Arkistant took a larger arkle out of the cupboard behind him and placed it on the table. The Arkists pushed their chairs back, stood up and began to Sing. The arkle rose from the table and floated up to near the ceiling. One by one, the Arkists ran out of breath and, as each stopped Singing, the arkle lost height. Finally, only one Arkist remained Singing and the arkle settled back down onto the table top. The Arkistant gravely passed this Arkist the staff of office.

'For you are now Arkistant,' said the old Arkistant.

'For I am now Arkistant,' said the new Arkistant, taking the staff.

Suddenly, I felt very sad for the Arkists. They once Sang of the Waves but their Song had dwindled to ritualised recreation. I could never live this life.

I was very tired and there was a dull ache in my larynx. I went through to my cubicle, rolled out my sleeping bag, undressed and got into bed. The bed was hard and lumpy. I tossed and turned until I found a comfortable pose and fell asleep.

I woke the next morning to a jaunty tune. I got up and dressed. The sitting room was empty. On the veranda, the new Arkistant was sitting in a rocking chair playing a reel on the pan pipes. When she had finished, she put the pipes down and smiled at me.

'There's warm water if you'd like to wash,' said the Arkistant. 'And there's food in the kitchen.'

'Thank you,' I said. 'What's doing?'

'You could sluice out the latrines,' said the Arkistant.

'All right,' I said, reluctantly. 'Where is everybody?'

'Working in the forest,' said the Arkistant.

'I thought Arkists didn't work,' I said.

'Of course we work!' said the Arkistant. 'How else would we eat?'

'But why do you become Arkists?' I asked. 'When you were Wave Singers, the Song was your work.'

The Arkistant stood up.

'We're all blinded by our Stretches,' she said, 'but we can't ever find them again. Once we recognise that the Waves are far stronger than our Songs, the Ark's the only shelter from the Great Flood.'

'But you don't have to find your Stretches again,' I insisted. 'There are other Stretches that can find you.'

'What would be the point?' said the Arkistant and wandered off round the veranda.

The latrines were under the Ark House, immediately below the shower drainage tank. I filled a bucket from the waste water spigot and mopped down the stalls and seats. Then I filled and emptied a bucket of waste water down the shaft of each closet.

When I'd finished, I returned upstairs. The Arkistant had gone and I was alone in the Ark House. I showered and helped myself to a bowl of lukewarm sadza from the pot on the stove. The sadza tasted slightly sour, but I was still very hungry despite all that I had eaten the night before. Then I washed up, gathered my things together, shut up the Ark House and set off for the Loch.

The Settlement was very busy. The burn through the Settlement was running high, driving the water wheel for the saw mill. Two teams were hauling logs out of the forest. At the mill, another team was feeding logs through the spinning blade, stacking the planks and sweeping up the fine shavings for pulping to make paper.

As I crossed the Settlement, nobody paid any attention to me. I walked back up onto the ridge and through the woods. When I reached the jetty, I saw the barge traversing the Loch, the wind filling the square green and orange-striped sail.

There was a flagpole on the landing stage at the end of the jetty. In the box at the base of the flagpole was a red and black flag. I raised the flag and stood and waved at the barge which changed course and came slowly towards me. As the barge pulled in along side of the landing stage, I lowered the flag and put it back in the box.

'On you get!' shouted the barge master, reaching out an arm.

I took her hand and jumped across. The barge left the jetty and headed back into the Loch. There were a dozen passengers but I didn't know any of them particularly well.

'What's doing?' I said to the barge master.
'It's a fine day,' said the barge master. 'Will you Sing for us?'
'What would you like me to Sing?' I asked.
'Suit yourself,' said the barge master.

I sat in the bow of the barge and pondered what to Sing. I didn't want to Sing a shanty or a round and I certainly didn't want to Sing my Stretch.

As I sat, I began to hear the barge ploughing through the water. Out in the centre of the Loch, with a steady breeze and a straight course, the barge Sang a cyclic Song. As the barge yawed and pitched so did its Song. Perhaps I could Sing with the barge.

I stood up in the bows facing the Loch. Relaxed and confident, I started to Sing. It was much easier to Sing with the barge than with the Loch.

When I stopped and turned around, the passengers were watching me closely. The passengers looked very unhappy. I left the bow and joined them.

'What's wrong?' I asked, concerned. 'Didn't you like the Song?'
'It didn't really feel right,' said a passenger.

'Why ever not?' I asked.

'It felt like you were just Singing for yourself,' said the passenger. 'Not for us.'

'But I meant to Sing for everyone,' I said.

'It wasn't like the usual Song,' said another passenger. 'It was different.'

'It was meant to be different,' I said. 'I wanted to try something new. What's wrong with that?'

'Your Song kept changing,' said the second passenger. 'How can we share a Song if we never know what's coming next?'

'But I was Singing with the barge!' I said. 'The barge's Song has got to change!'

'Maybe you should stick to Singing with other people,' said the first passenger.

'Yes,' said the second passenger. 'We want to hear the Song, not you.'

Admonished, I crossed the hold and sat in the stern, staring dejectedly at the wake of the barge. After a while, the barge master left the bridge and joined me.

'Well that was good,' she said. 'There's not many people know how to listen to the Loch. I really enjoyed that.'

'Nobody else did,' I replied, despondently. 'They said that I Sang for myself, not for them.'

'Well of course you did, didn't you,' said the barge master.

'I didn't mean to,' I said, defensively. 'They're just not used to hearing something different.'

'Maybe it's more than that,' said the barge master. 'Maybe they find it threatening.'

'Why should a new Song threaten anyone?' I asked.

'Life's been desperately hard,' said the barge master, patiently. 'Even now it's still really precarious. You know the Song helps hold us all together. It reminds us of what we could lose, as well as of what we've lost. If you challenge the Song then you challenge our stability.'

'So why didn't you all stop me then?' I asked. 'If it's *so* dangerous.'

The barge master laughed.

'It's not *so* dangerous,' she said. 'And you did Sing well.'

'I just wanted to sing a live Song,' I said. 'Not the echo of a dead one.'

'I wanted to do that too,' said the barge master. 'That's why I came to work on the barge.'

'You were a Singer?' I said, astonished.

'Oh yes,' said the barge master. 'A long time ago now.'

'Did you find your Stretch?' I asked.

'This is my Stretch,' said the barge master. 'It found me.'

'You know what I mean,' I said, petulantly.

'And you know what I mean,' said the barge master placidly.

'Why did you stop?' I asked.

'Who says I have?' said the barge master.

'I've never seen you at the Singings,' I said.

'I don't often leave the barge,' said the barge master.

'So where do you Sing?' I asked.

'On the barge, of course!' said the barge master.

The barge master climbed up onto the gunwale and sat with her legs dangling over the stern.

'Come on!' she said to me.

Gingerly, I joined her.

'What are we going to do?' I asked.

'Just listen,' said the barge master.

We sat quietly on the stern. All I could hear was the rush of the wake and the slap of the wash. Then I realised that the barge had a slight list. As the barge gently rolled, it Sang different Songs on either side.

'Well?' said the barge master.

'Maybe there are two Songs,' I said.

'Good!' said the barge master. She pointed to her left. 'I'll take the starboard. You try the port.'

The barge master started to Sing. She knew each movement of the barge and each response of the Loch. The barge master's Song was glorious. Where I had simply echoed the Song of the barge, she anticipated and challenged it. In awe, I sat and listened to the barge master.

Lucy

They said I should have a baby. So I said why. And they said it was my duty. I said what's all this duty crap, we're supposed to be anarchists. And they said that I should know by now that anarchy is about individual choices that benefit everyone.

All right then. So I got a bun in the oven. At least that was fun.

Then they said I wasn't supposed to sleep with just anyone. I should choose someone I could make a commitment with, someone who'd start a household with me.

And I got really cross and I said you want me to make choices and then you don't like them so tough. Of course I didn't just dance on the first hard-on I bumped into. Of course I thought about it; why do you think it took me so long? And why would I want to start a household with him? He's a drip. I'm in a household I like already, thank you very much. He can always come and live with us if he's so keen.

Still, they were nice to me as I grew bigger and bigger. I got better food and no one seemed to mind when I was too whacked to work. No one tells you how hard it is carrying a baby though, or how much it screws up your body. Just as well, really, or nobody would ever have any. And I hated being so dependent on everyone.

It was a huge relief when she finally came out. They said I was lucky, I'd had an easy birth. It didn't feel easy, that's for sure.

I said to them, here's your baby, I've carried her for

nine months and now I bloody well want to get on with my life. And they said, sorry mate, this is your life. She's your baby so you better look after her because no one else is going to do it for you. Sly bastards. Well of course I'm going to look after her, just not all the time.

At least his household's nice. They don't mind taking care of the baby. His dad goes all gooey over her. Shame he's stuck in that chair. That's where those big projects get you. One last heave and it'll all be perfect. Bollocks.

They keep asking me to move in with them but I couldn't hack it. It's all right for a couple of days but then it all gets a bit too cosy. What they like doing best is gossiping about each other. It really gets on my nerves. Why can't they just leave each other alone once in a while? Maybe that's why his mum bunks off to the Fort every day. She's a bit strange, what with all those books, but at least she doesn't try to tell me what to do, not like some people. And she does tell great stories.

His household's all upset about him vanishing but he'll be alright. He'll turn up when he's good and ready. He may be a drip but he's tough. He didn't cry out once when we got him off the moor and fixed his leg. He seemed more worried about doing something wrong. And he was so embarrassed when I had to help him pee. As if I'd never seen a prick before.

At least he knows what to do with it. If only he hadn't gone on and on afterwards, about me and him, and what I thought about him. I can see where that all comes from. How can anyone stand living like that?

No one seems to know why he took off though. His sister had the nerve to suggest it might be something to do with me but that's total crap. It's not as if we even know each other all that well. Anyway, what about his cousin in the Town? From what his sister says, she's pretty soft on him.

He does Sing beautifully. Why didn't he become a Wave Singer when he had the chance? People say Wave Singers have a good life. I wish I could learn to Sing like that. But I'd have to go to all those lessons with all the other drips. Maybe the baby'll learn to Sing. His dad would like that.

It's strange how we don't have an Ark or Singing. There must have been a huge bust-up when our lot split off and set up the Colony. I wonder why we ended up going with them? We were awfully young when our mother left. I don't really remember her. No one will talk about why she went. I'm not going to ask her.

And now they've started nagging me again about having another baby, as if one wasn't enough. Why don't they go on at my sister as well? All she cares about are her machines and trying to restart the satellite. I know I can't ever quite settle to anything the way she does. But that doesn't mean that all I'm good for is breeding.

Anyway, contacting the satellite makes a lot more sense than trying to build a great big power system from scratch. The satellite was supposed to give us loads of power. If only we could work out how to talk to it. But lots of people are frightened of what might happen if we start it up and it goes wrong again. What's the harm in trying? How could things be any worse?

At least he sees that. He asked his uncle about the satellite noises and he picked up how important it is to us. Och, maybe he's not so bad. . .

22 The barge master Sang steadily, voicing in and out of the starboard Song. Without halting her Singing, she reached across, tapped me on the shoulder and gestured over to her right. I knew I must join her. I sat up straight, faced the waves and Sang.

At first I concentrated on the wash on my side of the barge, echoing the port Song back across the water. As I Sang, I could hear how the port Song touched the starboard Song, like two adjacent Stretches in the Village Song. Cautiously, I began to echo strands of the barge master's Song into mine. The barge master looked across at me, smiled, and began to weave my Song back into hers. As we sat in the stern and Sang together, our twin Songs flowed and fused into a single Stretch.

When the sun was high over the barge, the barge master stopped Singing.

'I should give the helm a break,' said the barge master.

She stood up and walked back across the hold to the bridge. I stayed in the stern, watching the wake and listening to the wash.

This is how Singing should be. This is how I want to Sing.

Someone called me to join the others for lunch. My reverie broken, I returned to the main deck. Soup bubbled on the bargees' charcoal brazier. I wasn't very hungry and felt slightly queasy, but I couldn't refuse a bowl of the celery and chick pea broth. As we ate, we chatted politely. No one mentioned my Singing. Occasionally, I looked round for the barge master but she remained at the wheel.

After lunch the wind dropped. I felt bloated from lunch but I joined the others at the oars. As I rowed, I became increasingly aware of a deep churning sensation, low in my belly.

That evening, after we had tied up in the Village basin and the other passengers had disembarked, the barge master took me to one side.

'I really enjoyed Singing with you,' said the barge master. 'It's been a while since I've met anyone with your feel for it.'

'Are there others who Sing like that?' I asked, hopefully.

'Oh yes,' said the barge master.

'Do you ever Sing with each other?' I persisted.

'Not very often,' said the barge master. 'It's hard to arrange. You've just seen how other people react.'

'I'd like to Sing with you again,' I said. 'But I've no plans to go back to the Town.'

'You could come and join us on the barge,' said the barge master. 'There's always work. And there's lots I could teach you about Singing.'

Then I remembered a cautionary story my father once told us.

Siddhartha, a rich Brahmin, left his community and sought enlightenment as a wandering monk. Rejecting the Buddha's path through transcendence of suffering, he pursued base pleasure and personal gain.

How we all shuddered at this dreadful choice between religion and sybaritism.

Tiring of sensuality and abandoning his wife and child, Siddhartha became a ferryman, finally finding self-realisation in passive contemplation of the river.

How could anyone be so perverse? we asked. How could anyone be so selfish?

My father said that Siddhartha should have read *The Green*

Child. Then he'd have known that enlightenment lay in material reality and mutual aid. Then he'd have been a time traveller, said my mother, checking my fathers's scalp for dandruff, seeing as how *The Green Child* wasn't written for another two and a half thousand years.

It felt like an age since I'd last spoken with my mother but it was only a couple of days ago. We had left a lot unsaid.

'Thank you,' I said. 'But I've got to finish what I started.'

The barge master laughed.

'I bet you say that to all the girls,' she said. 'Haste ye back.'

The churning in my guts had started to ache. By the time I reached our house, the ache had turned to a painful griping.

I let myself into the house. My father was sitting by the fire, knitting.

'There you are!' said my father. 'I was just thinking about you. Have you eaten? There's still some food if you'd like some.'

'No thank you,' I said. 'I really don't feel so good.'

'You really don't look so good,' said my father, jovially. 'You must be worn out. Go and sleep it off. There's a bed made up in your old room.'

I hauled myself upstairs and lay down on the bed. The griping had turned to sharp spasms. I was hot and dizzy and couldn't settle. Suddenly, I felt as if my insides had liquefied. I stumbled downstairs to the outhouse where I passed out.

When I came to, I was slumped in a pool of my own excrement. I tried to get up but my legs wouldn't support me. I tried to call for help but all I could muster was a hopeless whimper. I passed out again.

When I next came to, it was dark outside and I was curled up in bed. My mother was sitting in a chair beside the bed, quietly watching me.

'How are you feeling?' said my mother.

'Pretty lousy,' I said, weakly. 'Could I have something to drink please?'

'Of course,' said my mother.

She poured a mug of water from the jug on the bedside table and held it out to me. I rolled over onto my side, took the mug and drank it down. My body shuddered as the water burnt through me cold and clear.

'Thank you,' I asked.

'How long have I been here?'

'Three days now,' said my mother.

'Have I been out of it all that time?' I asked.

'Dead to the world,' said my mother. 'Last night we heard you talking in your sleep. I thought you might be about to wake up but I couldn't rouse you.'

'What was I saying?' I asked.

'You were worried about the wild animals scrabbling at the door,' said my mother. 'You wanted them to break through the ice but you didn't want them to come any further.'

'Did I say anything else?,' I asked.

'You were talking to a girl,' said my mother. 'You were pleading with her to listen to you, begging her to give you another chance. Does that mean anything to you?'

Of course it meant something to me.

'Not much,' I said, evasively.

'I don't think it was Goode,' said my mother. 'She'd love you to stay with her and the bairn.'

'I must have been raving,' I said.

'You've been quite poorly,' said my mother. 'Don't you remember anything?'

'I'd just got back from the town,' I said. 'I felt really feverish and I desperately needed to shit.'

'You certainly managed that,' said my mother. 'When I found you, you were a right mess. I washed you down and then the twins helped me carry you upstairs. It looks like you've got some sort of food poisoning. Do you have any idea what you might have eaten?'

I told my mother about my journey back from the Town. As I recounted my visit to the Arkists, my mother became increasingly agitated.

'Well,' said my mother when I'd finished. 'I suppose I shouldn't have expected anything else of them. Sometimes they can be quite contemptible.'

'What do you mean?' I asked. 'They tried their best to help me.'

'They tried to impress you with cheap conjuring tricks,' said my mother, 'and then they poisoned you.'

'Don't be so harsh,' I said.

'You're surely not defending them?' said my mother.

'I'm sure they meant me no harm,' I said. 'And they showed me a way of Singing that I'd never seen before.'

'It's a snare and a delusion,' said my mother. 'And deep down you know that. Otherwise you'd have joined them.'

'I still could,' I said. 'There's nothing for me here.'

My mother's face fell.

'You're not serious,' she said. 'You can't be.'

'Why are you so critical of them?' I asked. 'Their Arkistant said that you'd written most of their texts. How can you help them if you dislike them so much?'

My mother looked directly at me.

'You've always known I was a pornographer,' said my mother. 'That's what I do.'

'But why?' I asked. 'Why write things you won't let us read?'

'I've told you lots of times,' said my mother. 'People need something to take their minds off how lousy their lives are. If they weren't provided with illicit pleasures, they'd just invent them for themselves. And whatever they come up with would probably be a lot more anti-social than Arkism.'

'But you always say that pornography demeans people,' I said. 'And exploits them. So how can you stand writing it?'

My mother looked at me sadly.

'It's all I can do,' she said finally.

'But you write beautifully!' I said. 'You tell wonderful stories. Why don't you write more things that you'd like to read yourself?'

'I can't anymore,' said my mother bitterly. 'Do you think I haven't tried? Everything I want to write's been written already by other people. Why do you think the house is full of books? Why do you think they're so precious to me?'

I didn't know what to say.

I sat up and tried to reach across for the water jug. The mug slipped out of my hand and fell loudly onto the floor. As my mother got up to retrieve the mug, a baby started to cry downstairs.

'Don't worry,' said my mother, examining the mug. 'It's not broken.'

'Who's that crying?' I asked my mother.

'That's your child,' said my mother.

'Is Goode here?' I asked, puzzled. 'The boat's not had enough time to make the round trip.'

'No,' said my mother. 'Goode's not here.'

'So how did Salvador get here?' I asked, confused.

'Who's Salvador?' asked my mother.

'Goode's son,' I said.

'Your son,' said my mother.

'Yes,' I said. 'My son. Our son.'

'That's an apt name,' said my mother. 'But that's not Salvador crying.'

'But you just told me it was my child crying,' I said.

'You'll see,' said my mother, smiling mischievously.

My mother got up and went downstairs.

I lay back on the bed, baffled and exhausted.

23 My mother returned and sat down, cradling a baby wrapped in a white woollen shawl. The baby looked as if it was about the same age as Salvador. My mother soothed the baby and gently unwrapped the shawl. The baby had bright red hair and large feet.

Oh.

My mother gently bounced the baby up and down. The baby stopped crying and smiled at me. When the baby smiled it looked like my mother. My parents said that when I was young I looked like my mother.

Oh.

'Is he really mine?' I asked.

'He's a she,' said my mother. 'Could she be yours?'

Of course she could.

'I suppose so,' I said.

'Jolly good!' said my mother. 'Not that it makes any difference,' she added hastily.

'What's she called?' I asked.

'They don't use names,' said my mother.

'What do you call her?' I asked.

'The baby,' said my mother.

I gazed at the baby. The baby looked so like the girl with red hair. I stared at the baby. The baby looked so like my mother. I thought of Salvador asleep in my arms.

'Can I hold her?' I asked.

'Best wait 'til you're up and about,' said my mother. 'We don't really know what's been wrong with you.'

'All right,' I said, 'but what's she doing here?'

'Why shouldn't she be here?' retorted my mother.

'Don't young babies need to be with their mothers?' I asked.

'Everyone needs to be with people who will care for them,' said my mother firmly.

'So where is her mother?' I persisted.

'Up on the moor, I expect,' said my mother.

'What's she doing up there?' I asked. 'What's more important than looking after her baby?'

'You'll need to ask her that yourself,' said my mother. 'Does it matter?'

Of course it didn't matter. Of course it mattered.

'How long has she been with you?' I asked.

'She first came around four months ago,' said my mother. 'But she's not here all the time. We take it in turns to look after her. We'd love to have her for longer. I'd forgotten how nice it is to have a baby in the house. Maybe you could have another one.'

Maybe.

'There's time enough,' I said evasively.

'No there isn't,' said my mother heatedly. 'There's nothing like time enough. Your father and I won't be here for ever and none of you show much sign of house-holding.'

'What about my sister?' I asked.

'That'll not last,' said my mother. 'We're expecting her back any time now. He's a nice enough lad but ever so dull. What about yourself?'

'What about myself?' I said guardedly.

'It looks like you're spoiled for choice.' said my mother. 'If you're not happy here why don't you go and live with Goode?'

'I don't think that would work,' I said. 'We all know each other too well.'

'So why don't you join your friend in the Colony?' asked my mother.

'I thought she was with the boy who helped me,' I said. 'Couldn't he be the baby's father?'

'Don't be so daft,' said my mother, affectionately.

'Why's that daft?' I asked.

'That's enough for now,' said my mother, standing up. 'You should get some rest.'

After my mother left, I dozed fitfully. I wanted to sleep but the questions didn't. Why was I daft? Was he her brother? Brothers sire bairns. Why was I daft? Was he gay? Gays sire bairns. Why was I daft?

What was the Project? Was Wavesinging part of it? Was that why Rufus was so despondent when he discovered that Salvador was deaf? He'd implied that very few people survived the Event. So everyone in our community must be related and so the girl with red hair must be related to me. My mother implied that the Project passed from parent to child. The girl with red hair could Sing. Maybe Wavesinging passed from parent to child. Could the baby be the Project?

And what were the creatures that haunted the dry Firth? The woman with the brand on her forehead thought they were something to do with the Project. The creatures left handprints in the snow. The woman had said that they liked her Singing. Could the creatures be related to us?

I turned and tossed and finally fell asleep.

When I next woke, I was sticky with sweat but the fever had gone. I slowly got out of bed and stretched. I felt weak and hungry but my head was still bursting with questions. I pulled on the dressing gown that was hanging over the bedside chair and went cautiously downstairs.

My father was sitting at the kitchen table peeling potatoes.

'You're up at last,' he said. 'That's a relief. We were worried about you. You haven't been so ill since you were a wee lad.'

I looked round the kitchen.

'Where's the baby?' I asked.

'Gone back to the Colony,' said my father.

'Already?' I said. 'I thought she'd only just got here.'

'Oh no,' said my father. 'She's been here for a couple of weeks now.'

'I didn't see her when I first came back,' I said.

'She was sleeping,' said my father.

'Why didn't you tell me about her?' I asked.

'There seemed to be more important things to talk about,' said my father. 'And you left so quickly.'

'Was she here?' I asked.

'Was who here?' said my father.

'The baby's mother,' I said.

'She came first thing this morning,' said my father.

'Was anyone with her?' I asked.

'Not that I noticed,' said my father.

'Did she say anything?' I asked.

'Not a lot,' said my father. 'Though she did ask why you hadn't been to see her.'

'Didn't you tell her I was unwell?' I asked.

'I expect I mentioned it,' said my father, plainly enjoying himself.

'Why didn't she come and see me?' I asked.

'How do you know she didn't?' said my father. 'You were asleep, weren't you?'

'So she did come and see me,' I said, irritated with my father's deliberate obtuseness.

'Don't get so worked up about it,' said my father, airily. 'Go and have a shower. You'll feel a lot better.'

Why was my father in such a good mood?

The shower was tepid but it revived me. I dried myself and went back upstairs to the bedroom and checked the cupboards. My clothes were still hanging in the wardrobe and folded neatly in the chest of drawers, just as I'd left them a lifetime ago. I dressed and went downstairs.

'You must be hungry,' said my father, grating the potatoes. 'I was going to make latkes for lunch.'

'I still feel a bit delicate,' I said.

'There's some yoghurt in the larder,' said my father. 'Let's see if that'll settle you.'

He trundled across the kitchen and spooned yoghurt into a bowl from an earthenware jar.

'Would you like anything in it?' said my father. 'I could chop you some dried apricots. Or stir in some honey'

'No thank you,' I said. 'I'll just try it on its own.'

I took the bowl and sat down to eat. The yoghurt was thick and creamy, with a soft, sour aftertaste.

'That was really good,' I said, scraping round the bowl. 'Where did it come from?'

'Your friend brought it,' said my father. 'She usually brings us something from the Colony.'

'Usually?' I said. 'When's she coming back?'

'Not for a while, I expect,' said my father. 'You could always go and see her.'

Maybe.

'What day is it?' I asked.

'Market day,' said my father. 'She always brings the baby and collects it on market day.'

'Always?' I asked. 'How often has the baby been here?'

'Lots of times,' said my father.

'Lots of times?' I echoed.

'Oh yes,' said my father. 'Every couple of weeks.'

'Isn't she still breast feeding?' I asked.

'Obviously not!' said my father.

'Isn't she a bit young to be weaned?' I asked.

'She's not exactly wasting away,' said my father.

I took the bowl over to the sink and rinsed it out.

'Does she talk about me?' I asked.

'Isn't she a bit young to be talking?' said my father.

'Not the baby,' I said crossly.

'I know that,' said my father. 'Of course she talks about you.
We all do. What do you expect, just disappearing like that.'

'That's not what I meant,' I said.

'I know that,' said my father. 'So you do like her then?'

Of course I like her.

'She's all right, I suppose,' I said.

'All right enough to make babies,' said my father, pointedly.

Was that what we did? Was that all we did?

'Aren't you going to the market?' I asked.

'I thought I'd better stay here with you,' said my father.

If she came every market day then maybe she would still be at
the Fort.

'We could go together,' I said.

'Are you sure you're up to it?' asked my father.

'I think a wee jaunt might do me good,' I said.

'But you're only just out of bed,' said my father.

'Let's give it a go,' I said. 'Which wheelchair?'

'Number one!' said my father firmly.

24 My father's second best wheelchair had been assembled from spare parts from the Store. This small, lightweight chair manoeuvred easily inside the house. My father's favourite was a mahogany bathchair with a wooden tiller. He said that it lent him a certain gravitas. It certainly weighs enough, said my mother, twirling his villainous moustache with beeswax.

I retrieved the bathchair from its shed behind the house. Then I helped my father into the chair.

'What are we taking?' I asked my father.

'Let's not bother,' said my father. 'There's nothing we need and if we don't take anything we won't have to open up the booth.'

We set off through the Village towards the Fort, the bathchair's wheels rattling on the wooden slats of the boardwalk. By the time we reached the steps that led up to the Fort, I was weary from pushing my father.

My father rummaged in the wire basket under the bathchair.

'Here you are,' he said, proffering me the sling.

I looked at the sling and looked at my father. He had felt much heavier than I had remembered.

'I don't think I can manage you on my own,' I said. 'Would you mind if we just went back to the house?'

'No need,' said my father, airily. 'Why don't you drop me off at the midden. It's just round the corner. You can go to the market yourself. Find your mother and come back for me when you're done.'

I pushed my father along the stony path that hugged the side of the South Dyke. When we reached the midden hut, the woman with the brand on her forehead came out to greet us.

'Hello,' said the woman to my father. 'I've not seen you for a while. Are you stopping off?'

Why didn't she ask me to join them?

'Off you go,' said my father to me. 'See you later.'

I made my way back to the steps and climbed up to the Fort. The Parade Ground was very busy. Most of the booths were open. On the far side of the Parade Ground, I could see a crowd gathered around my mother. I wasn't in the mood for my mother's stories. I slowly worked my way round the booths, half-heartedly chatting with the people I met.

All the time I was watching out for the girl with the red hair and large feet. I yearned to see her again: there were so many things I wanted to ask her. I dreaded seeing her again: there were so many things I didn't want to hear.

The Wave Singers came down the main aisle of the Fort, stopped in the centre of the Parade Ground, formed a circle facing outwards and started to Sing. People left the booths and formed another circle around the Wave Singers. Drawn by the Song, but wary of the Wave Singers, I lingered by the booths.

From across the Parade Ground, the oldest Wave Singer gestured to me to join them. Everyone turned to look at me. Awkward and embarrassed, I smiled back but didn't move. The oldest Wave Singer left the group and came across to me.

'Come and Sing with us!' said the oldest Wave Singer, enthusiastically.

'I haven't Sung for far too long,' I told her.

'Then this is a good time to start again,' said the oldest Wave Singer.

'I'm really not ready,' I said.

'There's not so much time until the next Autumn Singing,' said the oldest Wave Singer. 'If you don't join us soon I'll have to choose someone else.'

'I can't join you,' I said. 'I know I can't.'

'But think of all the things you could learn,' said the oldest Wave Singer.

She took her £50 coin from her pocket and Sang it off her hand. I took the largest arkle from my bag, straightened it and Sang it across to her.

'Ah well,' said the oldest Wave Singer sadly, catching the arkle. 'Ah well.'

She handed me back the arkle and rejoined the other Wave Singers.

On the far side of the Parade Ground, the crowd surrounding my mother burst into applause and began to noisily disperse. Crossing the Parade Ground, I reached her as she was putting her notebook back into her satchel.

'Should you be here?' asked my mother.

'I'm alright,' I said.

'Where's your father?' asked my mother.

'Visiting the woman in the midden hut,' I said. 'He said we were to go and get him when we're ready. What are you up to now?'

'I'm going home,' said my mother, 'but I need to pick up some books from the office. Do you want to come with me?'

I was intrigued by my mother's invitation; she rarely asked anyone to visit the office.

We walked together down the centre of the Parade Ground, past the complex of old barracks and workshops, to the Ordnance Store. The office my mother used was on the third floor, looking out over the old Fort Major's House. We went into the Ordnance Store, climbed the stairs and entered a long straight corridor.

The corridor echoed to music. Intrigued by the music, I stopped to listen. It had a mechanical sound but was far more melodious than the wind chimes in the village on the Loch.

'Come on!' said my mother, walking quickly away from me.

I followed my mother to the far end of the corridor and into the office.

The office was poorly lit and very cluttered. Battered filing cabinets with open drawers stood on either side of the door. Floor to ceiling shelves on the side walls were stuffed haphazardly with books and folders. A long table ran along the windowed wall opposite the door. An Underwood typewriter stood on the table, surrounded by more piles of books and papers. My mother fossicked in the piles and handed me the occasional book which I put into her bag.

'There's a couple more that I need from the library' said my mother. 'Just wait here. I'll not be long.'

My mother disappeared through the door. I sat down in the wooden armchair and idly surveyed the table. As I browsed the piles of books and papers, I began to realise that they were considerably more organised than at first appearance. Each pile was surmounted with a brown manila folder, neatly labelled with a title and starting date. Most of the dates preceded my birth.

One folder was labelled *Genealogies*. I picked it up and opened it. The folder was full of kinship diagrams. On most of the diagrams, the upper nodes were marked with question marks but some of the lower nodes and leaves bore names I recognised.

I flicked through the pages until I spotted one with my and my siblings' names. Then I followed the branches up from our names and found my parents. My mother was linked to Rufus, who was linked to Sally, with branches down to our cousins. There was a freshly drawn link from my name to Goode's, with a branch down to Salvador.

There was also a freshly drawn link from my name to an unnamed leaf and yet another branch down to another unnamed leaf at the same level as Salvador's. These must be for the girl with the red hair and our child. Another link led from the girl with red hair to a sibling.

'Well there's a surprise,' said my mother, who was standing in the doorway watching me.

'So she does have a brother,' I said, nervously.

'A sister,' said my mother.

'A sister?' I echoed lamely.

'Yes,' said my mother. 'They're twins.'

'Who's their mother?' I asked.

'The woman in the midden hut,' said my mother.

'The woman in the midden hut,' I repeated dumbly. 'Why didn't you tell me?'

'We didn't think we'd ever see her again,' said my mother. 'Anyway, why do think your father likes visiting her so much?'

'I hadn't really thought about it,' I said. 'They're obviously friends.'

'They're more than friends,' said my mother.

'How can they be more than friends?' I asked, increasingly confused.

'Have another look,' said my mother.

I followed the branches up from my father and from the woman with the brand on her forehead. Both branches led to the same parents.

'She's his sister!' I said. 'Why didn't you tell us we had more family?'

'We don't have families,' said my mother. 'Remember?'

If the girl with red hair and big feet was my cousin, then maybe our child was another link in the Project.

'Can she Sing?' I asked my mother.

'That's a good question!' said my mother. 'Yes, she was an excellent Singer. Just like your grandparents.'

'But my father can't Sing,' I said.

'No,' said my mother. 'He's a dreadful Singer. You know it's not just simply inherited.'

The girl with the red hair had learnt my Song so quickly. I wondered if our child could Sing. A part of me hoped that she couldn't.

'So where's the other twin?' I asked.

'She's in the Colony,' said my mother. 'You've met her. She brought you home after you broke your leg.'

'But I thought it was a boy who helped me,' I said.

'Yes,' said my mother. 'Lots of people do.'

Sister, brother, what's the difference if she prefers their company to mine.

'We should get going,' said my mother, again.

'Can I take it with me?' I asked, pointing to *Genealogies*.

'I'd rather you didn't,' said my mother. 'It's the only one and I don't want your father folding it into arkles. You can borrow this though.'

My mother reached across the table and handed me a thin folder. The folder was inscribed:

A True History of the Project.

My mother's name was underneath the title.

'Are you sure?' I asked my mother.

'Oh yes,' said my mother. 'There are lots more copies.'

'Why didn't you show me it before?' I asked.

'I'm showing it to you now,' said my mother. 'Let's be off.'

I picked up *A True History of the Project* and put it my bag with the X-FLR6 manual.

Clara

The boat's listing a wee bit to port. Not much. No one else has noticed. But I can hear the change in her Song.

I can't see anything amiss from inside the hold. She's probably snagged something. I suppose I could go down and have a look at the hull but it's pretty hopeless in this murky water. I hope she hasn't sprung a strake.

Maybe we could use one of the locks as a dry dock. We could lower her down onto blocks. But we'd have to drain the lock and set the blocks and fill the lock and hope the blocks stayed in place. And then when we'd finished we'd have to drain the lock and remove the blocks. Docks, locks, blocks. It'll all take too long. And I'm not even sure if the gates will keep the water out for long enough if she needs major repairs.

I suppose we'll have to get her onto dry land. There used to be a stack of rollers at the Town Quay but I've not seen them for ages. Someone's bound to have found a better use for them.

I hate it when she's out of the water. I loathe sleeping ashore: I feel shipwrecked, marooned, cast away.

You know where you are on the water. The waves don't lie.

I don't feel safe sleeping on shore. The others tease

me about it. Kindly, mind. They can't wait to get
back to their households. The boat's my household.

Lots of people say I should name her. Why is
everyone so obsessed with naming? The Villagers
want to give everything a name. The Colonists
don't want to name anything. I'm not a Colonist
but there's only one boat so why does she need a
name? Grace says she should be named after one of
the great boats of the myths: 'Karaboudjan',
'Lurking Wolf', 'Sirius', 'Oshun Oxtra', 'Unicorn'.

Why should I name her? She isn't my boat even if
she's my household. If I drown tomorrow, someone
else will sail her the day after.

They say drowning's a peaceful way to go, once you
stop fighting the waves.

You can trust the waves. You can't trust people.

I suppose in a way she is my boat. I know her best. No
one's crewed her as long as I have. Some of them find
me too cranky. Some of them are frightened of the
water.

It's curious how people worry about what's beneath the
Loch. There aren't any mythical beasts, except in
Grace's tales.

I am a maid upon the land, I am a silkie in the sea.

And we are our own monsters.

It was Grace that found me. I was barely conscious.
He'd knocked me about badly. He'd really wanted
to hurt me.

We'd known each other since childhood. He'd

wanted me to leave the boat and set up household. He pushed and pushed, so I tried staying with him when the boat was docked.

I quickly felt trapped by him. He was so jealous of my life on the water. I wanted him to join the crew but he said I couldn't be his master and his housemate and he didn't want a master.

I'm no master, no matter what they call me. But you can't run a boat by consensus. Everyone knows how skilled I am. No one else has my experience though anyone can acquire it. Why should someone be penalised because they're good at something?

I thought we'd parted on good terms. I can see now that he thought we'd parted on my terms.

They found him on the Quay. Why was he just sitting there on a bollard as if nothing had happened? He was covered in bruises and scratches where I'd tried to drive him off.

I was terrified that I might be pregnant. Grace helped me make sure I wasn't. Nobody said anything though I knew they all disapproved. It was my choice. We like to think that every child is precious but I couldn't bear the fruit of his hate.

I didn't see them cast him out. They say he was calm until they took out the knife. I hope he suffered. I hope I'll never see him again.

For ages, I couldn't leave the boat. Grace was so good to me. She was kind and patient long after most people seemed to have forgotten what he'd done to me. No one ever talked about it. Maybe they were embarrassed. Or ashamed.

Poor Grace. She's the most trapped of all of us. Not

by her life but by her imagination. She sees so many possibilities yet knows why they can't be realised.

I think I'd have gone crazy without my Singing. It's wonderful that Grace's eldest wants to Sing with me. He's a nice lad. He's not drifting, he's driven though he doesn't yet know it. Of course he's not content with finding his Stretch, he wants to know what happens next. Just like I did.

I do wish I could persuade him to join the crew. When we Sing together, I know that we're both hearing exactly the same weird weave of our Songs with the boat's and the Loch's. A fair wind and floating free. Singing with the waves, not for them. I think I feel more at ease with him than just about anyone else. . .

25 We left the office and set off back down the corridor. As we neared the middle of the corridor, the sound of the music grew louder.

'What is that music?' I asked my mother.
'Papageno's bells,' said my mother. 'I'll show you.'

She stopped and opened a door.

'In we go,' said my mother.

I followed my mother into a room shelved with deep racks full of machines. In the centre of the room was a large table covered with mechanical devices in various states of disrepair. Above the table, a rotating shaft ran the length of the room,

In the centre of the table was a wooden box with an open lid. From the side of the box, a pulley was connected to the shaft by a belt.

I walked over to the box to take a closer look.

Rising from a mirrored base in the centre of the box, a pink manikin in a frilly dress turned round and round as the music played. The twirling doll was reflected over and over again between the base and the mirrored lid.

'Just like a ballerina!' said my mother. 'Isn't it pleasing!'
'It's grand!' I said. 'Can it play different tunes?'
'I suppose there might be more movements somewhere,' said my mother.
'What's the movement?' I asked.

My mother unlatched the front of the box and folded it down.

Inside, the pulley drove a small drum covered in studs. As the drum rotated, the studs brushed the ends of the tines of a metal comb, sounding the notes.

'Could I set up a movement myself?' I asked.

'I don't see why not,' said my mother. 'Come in and use the workshop. What do you have in mind.'

'I wonder if I could make it Sing,' I said.

'Oh no,' said my mother. 'The sound it makes is far too regular. Come on.'

We left the Fort and went down the steps to the midden path.

'Do you remember the last time we were here?' asked my mother, as we rounded the South Dyke.

'It must have been just before I found my Stretch,' I said.

'Do you regret not joining the Wave Singers?' asked my mother.

'There's time yet,' I said.

My mother looked crestfallen. Suddenly I felt sorry for my mother.

'No,' I said. 'Of course I don't regret it.'

'That's a relief,' said my mother. 'It would be a terrible waste.'

'A waste of what?' I asked guardedly, unsure if this was a compliment.

'We'll see,' said my mother. 'Look, here's your father.'

My father was sitting in his best wheelchair outside the midden hut.

'You took long enough!' said my father, as my mother bent over to kiss him.

'How is she?' asked my mother, putting her bag in my father's lap.

'Well enough,' said my father. 'You should have come earlier. You both just missed the girl from the Colony.'

'Her daughter was here?' I exclaimed.

My father looked quizzically at my mother. My mother just shrugged.

'She left around ten minutes ago,' said my father.

'Perhaps I could catch her up,' I said.

'Maybe if you're quick,' said my father. 'She's got the bairn on her back which'll slow her down a bit.'

I took the path through the Village and onto the dunes. In the distance, silhouetted against the sky, I could see the girl with the red hair and large feet crossing the ridge. I was cautious as I climbed the dunes. I was eager to join her but I didn't want to break my leg again. As the dunes grew steeper, I lost sight of the girl. When I reached the ridge, there was no sign of her.

Rather than following the winding path, I set off directly across the moor. At first, the ground was level and the purple heather was firm underfoot. But as I neared the centre of the moor, the ground became less even and increasingly boggy. I wanted to head straight for the Colony but I kept having to skirt round the glistening pools of oily water. I felt disheartened by my lack of progress. Reluctantly, I turned away from the marshes.

Making my way back towards the line of the path, I began to hear faint snatches of a voice carried on the breeze. As I neared the path, I realised that the voice bore a strangely familiar dodecahedron Corner Song. The Song was based on my Neap Tide Stretch.

Eagerly, I joined the path. As I approached the Colony, the Song grew louder. At the entrance to the Colony, I saw the girl with red hair and large feet sitting on a bench. The baby's toes curled as it suckled at the bottle.

The girl with red hair stopped Singing.

'What kept you,' said the girl with red hair.

'I got here as fast as I could,' I said.

'It doesn't take a year to get here,' said the girl.

'I've been away,' I said defensively. 'And I've been ill.'

'I know that, said the girl. 'Come and meet your daughter.'

She held the baby out to me.

'I've met her already,' I said, taking the baby.

I sat down on the bench and cradled the baby on my lap.

'What do you want to call her?' asked the girl with red hair.

'I thought you didn't use names,' I said.

'We don't,' said the girl. 'But you do.'

'I've no idea,' I said helplessly.

'Try!' said the girl with red hair.

'Siloën,' I said without thinking.

'That's a strange name for a baby,' said the girl. 'All right then. Siloën. But I'm still going to call her 'the baby'. So where's her present?'

'What present?' I asked, surprised.

'Her present!' said the girl, insistently. 'We give babies presents, not names.'

'I don't think I've got anything suitable,' I said.

'She doesn't need anything suitable,' said the girl. 'Babies don't really need anything at all. That's hardly the point.'

I rummaged desperately in my bag with a free hand.

'Would she like this?' I asked, taking out the smallest arkle.

'I don't know,' said the girl. 'Why don't you offer it to her?'

I sat the arkle on the palm of my hand and gently sang to it. The arkle rose from my palm. The girl looked at me strangely. The baby gurgled and reached out for the arkle. A sudden breeze whipped the arkle away over the Colony. The baby stiffened and began to mewl.

'Well that's no use to her now,' said the girl, holding out her arms for the baby. 'Have you got anything else?'

I returned the baby to the girl and reached into the backpack.

'I brought this for you,' I said, showing the X-FLR6 manual to the girl with red hair. 'But you could share it.'

'What's it about?' said the girl.

'It tells us how to talk to the satellite,' I said.

I opened the manual.

'Have a look at this,' I said, showing the girl with red hair the page for the Primary Startup Sequence

'But it doesn't make any sense,' said the girl, glancing at the page. 'It's just lots of letters and numbers.'

'It's a code,' I said. 'Listen.'

I started to whistle the sounds we had heard on the radio. As I whistled, I ran a finger down the column of codes.

The girl looked thoughtful.

'Hmmm,' she said pensively. 'Could you do the sequence you heard in the Town?'

I whistled the response from the disk Rufus had played me.

The girl suddenly smiled in recognition.

'It's just like reading music!' said the girl. 'Can you do any more of it?'

'I've tried and tried,' I said. 'But I can't work out how to turn the codes into sounds.'

'Hmmm,' said the girl. 'Pass it over. I'll swap you.'

She handed the baby back to me and picked up the manual.

I sat quietly, gently rocking the baby on my shoulder, while the girl with red hair studied the manual.

'Hmmm,' said the girl. 'Maybe we could work out how to generate the sounds from the codes.'

She closed the manual and sat still, staring out across the moor.

'Hmmm,' said the girl. 'Maybe we could construct a transmitter and try to talk to the satellite.'

The girl with red hair and large feet got up.

'Where are you going?' I asked.

'I need to talk to her about this,' said the girl.

'Who do you need to talk to?' I asked, baffled.

'My twin,' said the girl. 'Who else do you think I meant?'

'What about the baby?' I asked.

'What about her?' replied the girl, puzzled.

'Don't you want to take her with you?' I asked.

'Not particularly,' said the girl.

'What should I do with her?' I asked.

'She's just had a big feed so she'll not want to eat for a while,' said the girl. 'You could try putting her down to sleep. We're still in the same hut.'

She pointed across the Colony at a brightly painted wooden house with smoke rising from the chimney.

'So can I stay here for a bit?' I asked, hopefully.

The girl looked at me strangely.

'Of course you can,' she said. 'Who else is going to look after the baby?'

26 The girl with red hair and large feet walked away, clutching the X-FLR6 manual. I crossed the Colony in the opposite direction and entered the hut. The wall of ticking clocks still dominated the main room but the other end was now partitioned off by a woollen curtain. Behind the curtain was a wooden cot mounted on metal rockers. I laid the baby down in the cot and covered her with a blanket. Then I sat and gently rocked the cot, Singing softly to the baby.

When the baby was asleep, I got up and went through the main room to the kitchen. A mutton and vegetable stew was bubbling in a large pot on the cast-iron range. I was very hungry but I felt cautious about eating anything so rich. There was a bowl of pears on the kitchen table. I found a knife in the drawer in the table and cut a pear into quarters. Then I carefully excised the pear seeds and put them with the others in the shallow dish next to the bowl. I took the kettle outside and filled it with water from the tank in front of the hut. Moving the stew pot to one side, I placed the kettle beside it on the range.

I heard a muted bleat from beyond the kitchen and quickly went back through to the main room. The baby was fast asleep. I looked out of the rear window. The girl with red hair sat on a stool milking a goat tethered to a stake.

I sat next to the cot, slowly eating the pear, savouring every bite. I hadn't eaten a pear since I was a child.

When I had finished, I took *A True History of the Project* out of the bag and began to read:

0.   Introduction

Constructing a history relies entirely on the interpretation of evidence. Thus, the assertion that any one History is True may seem somewhat impertinent: evidence is never complete and interpretation is always partisan. Here I can do no more than assert both the low probability of any new evidence coming to light and that I have honestly tried to distinguish clearly matters of record from my own opinions. Nonetheless, if anyone wishes to verify the accuracy of this account, the entire known written record of our community is publicly accessible as a unitary collection.

1.   The Project – an Overview

The Project may best be understood as a series of concurrent yet longitudinal mythopoeic contrivances that serve to:

i)   shape individuated rites of passage for its unknowing neophytes, who unwittingly contribute fundamentally to their formation;

ii)   provide a non-antagonistic conduit for such neophytes to rehearse and resolve their contradictions;

iii)   bond its knowing adepts, enhancing social cohesion.

The origins of The Project are obscure. One popular theory holds that the first Project was an elaborate practical joke.

In its current form, The Project exhibits the following characteristics:

a)   adepts are of an older generation than neophytes;

b)   a neophyte's first awareness of The Project occurs when they overhear its mention by adepts;

c)   adepts' responses to questions about The Project are often evasive, or even contradictory, but imply confirmation of neophyte suspicions, hence encouraging the framing of further questions;

d)   thus, through cycles of questions and answers, each neophyte takes an active but unconscious part in elaborating their own instance of The Project;

e)   when a neophyte's interest in The Project declines, or becomes antagonistic, they are made aware of The Project's true nature and function. . .

So I had been duped. There was no Project. Or rather, there were many Projects, in particular the one I had contrived for myself.

I had first overheard my mother and Rufus mention The Project in the Town. I had asked Goode about The Project; she had thought it involved escape from our society's cul-de-sac. My mother had deflected all mention of The Project and denied that Goode knew anything about it. Of course, Goode only knew of her own Project not mine, but Goode knowing anything about The Project, and my mother's denial of her knowledge, had confirmed its existence for me.

Goode bearing Salvador had ended her Project but had inflamed mine. I had steadily constructed my own Project as selective breeding for a more and more highly evolved Song. When I returned from the dry Firth, my mother had further confirmed my Project by implying that our genetic line embodied it. But then Rufus had said that The Project no longer mattered. Was that why my mother chose to enlighten me now?

But had I been duped? The Project had led me to question Wave Singing and to new forms of Song. And The Project had led me to find the X-FLR6 manual.

A small clear voice deep in my head told me that now I was duping myself. Finding the manual had nothing to do with The Project and everything to do with the girl with crazed red hair and large feet.

I felt angry and cheated and hollow.

The kettle's whistle shook me from my tangled reverie. The kettle's whistle woke the baby who mewled and sucked her thumb. I put *A True History of the Project* back into the bag. Then I picked up the baby and returned to the kitchen. The girl was sitting at the table with her twin.

'Pass her over,' she said.

The girl and her twin watched me silently as I took the kettle off the range and made a pot of matte.

'So what do you think we should do?' I asked despondently, giving them each a cup of tea.

'Well,' said the twin. 'It should be straightforward to convert a radio to a transmitter, and to link it to a receiver so they're both always operating on the same wavelength. Then we could make oscillator circuits to generate the sounds, once we've worked out how they're linked to the codes. The hard bit will be producing the sounds in the right order. The whole thing would be so easy if we could run a computer but it'd take months to set one up and there's no way we can produce enough electricity continuously for that length of time.'

'What about the sheep?' I asked, sarcastically.

'We gave up on the sheep,' said the twin, simply. 'We couldn't ever keep them moving for more than a couple of minutes and

242

whenever they got a chance they kept trying to smash their way out of the wheel.'

I sat cradling the mug in my hands, watching the steam swirl across the surface of the matte. The sounds were repetitive; I thought about the gamelan band and the wind driven chimes and the dancer rotating on the music box.

'Maybe you could build a machine to generate the sounds,' I said finally. 'Maybe you could make a music box movement to produce them.'

'How would that work?' asked the twin.

I tried to explain. My explanation was punctuated repeatedly by pointed questions.

'It's just not feasible,' said the girl with red hair when I'd finished. 'It would be hard enough to get the notes to sound true. Then we'd have to make sure that they played for just the right length of time and that they didn't overlap.'

'Hmmm,' said the twin. 'We could maybe use a movement to trigger switches for the oscillators in the right order. A bit like a washing machine control unit. It wouldn't have to be anything like as accurate as a musical movement.'

The twin took a piece of charcoal from the range and began to draw diagrams on the kitchen table.

I spent the next two weeks in the Colony. Most of the time I kept to myself, houseworking and minding the baby. Most of the time the girl with red hair treated me with polite contempt, much like the other Colonists. Sometimes the girl with red hair invited me into her bed. But the twin and I spent every afternoon working on linking the sounds to the codes.

On the first afternoon, the twin observed that, while I only knew a few of the sounds that would be needed for the whole primary startup sequence, the sound was directly related to the value of its code: the bigger the code value the higher the note. If we could find the frequency of any one sound, then we could work out how to calculate the frequencies of all the others.

I told the twin that I really didn't understand what she was telling me. The twin patiently reminded me that the note played by a chime or whistle gets higher as the length of its tube gets shorter. And as a note gets higher, its frequency gets bigger so you could find the frequency of a note if you knew its wavelength. She gave up trying to explain to me how you could make an electronic circuit to generate a particular note if you could make a coil with the right number of turns of wire for the note's frequency.

I spent much of the second afternoon whistling just one note until my lips and cheeks ached. Meanwhile, the twin painstakingly trimmed a length of metal tubing until it sounded true when struck with a small hammer. She then measured the length of the pipe, worked out the frequency of the note it sounded and calculated how many turns of wire were needed to make a coil for the oscillator circuit.

On the third afternoon, the twin wound a coil, mounted it with scrap electrical components on a circuit board, and rigged it up to the bicycle generator and a loud speaker. I then mounted the bicycle generator and pedalled while she adjusted the circuit until it sounded the same note as the metal chime.

On the fourth afternoon, the twin used a Brunsvega mechanical calculator to work out how many turns of wire were needed for the coil for each code's sound. After she completed each calculation, she double checked it and I wrote down the result. At the end of the fourth afternoon, we had a table of all the codes we needed and the numbers of turns of wire for their coils.

At the end of two weeks, we had built enough oscillator circuits for all the notes in the primary startup sequence.

'What shall we do next?' I asked the twin.

'I'll start making the switch movement,' said the twin.

'Is there anything I can do to help?' I asked.

'Not really,' said the twin. 'It's a job for one person.'

'How long do you think it will take you?' I asked.

'I'm not sure,' said the twin. 'At least another three weeks.'

'I could always stay until you've finished,' I said tentatively.

'Of course you could,' said the twin, 'but she's getting more and more tetchy with you around.'

By now I didn't need to ask the twin who she was talking about.

'I suppose I might as well go back to the Village,' I said sadly.

'That's not such a bad idea,' said the twin. 'I'll let you know when we're ready to try the whole thing out.'

'Will you tell her I've gone?' I asked, pathetically.

'You can tell her yourself,' said the girl with red hair, who had come into the hut through the door behind me. 'Would you like to take the baby with you?'

'Wouldn't you miss her?' I asked.

'Of course,' said the girl.

'Would you come and see us?' I asked, hopefully.

'Of course,' she said.

'All right then,' I said. 'I'll be off.'

The girl with red hair gathered up all the baby's things. We walked across the Colony to the cable car. Then they helped me and the baby into the sling and launched us back down the cliff to the Village.

'Good bye,' said the girl with red hair and large feet as we sedately soared into space.

I was sad to leave. I was glad to leave.

27 Late one afternoon, I was hoeing the maize with the baby on my back. I had found a good rhythm and was Singing as I hoed. My father called me from the house. I was reluctant to stop; there were only another four rows to go. Then my father called me again. He sounded urgent so I finished the row and walked back to the house.

'There's a message for you from the Colony!' said my father, excitedly.

'What's the message?' I asked.

'They want you to get up there as soon as you can,' he said.

'Who brought the message?' I asked.

'I didn't know them,' said my father. 'They said they were on their way to the Fort.'

'Did they say anything else?' I asked.

'They said to tell you that they won't start without you,' said my father, 'but they're really keen to get going,'

'What about the baby?' I asked. 'She's not due back for another week.'

'They didn't mention Siloën,' said my father. 'Leave her with me.'

I walked to the Colony, my brain a jumble of musings.

It was a fine evening. The ground was firm and dry underfoot. I made good progress up the hill and across the moor.

I had been in the Village for several months. It had taken the twin far longer than she had expected to construct the switch movement. I had not been back to the Colony.

Dusk was falling.

I had grown surprisingly fond of the baby. The girl with red hair and large feet had come to collect or return the baby every couple of weeks. I missed the baby when she was in the Colony.

Venus appeared low on the horizon.

I rarely saw my mother. I had little to say to my father, who had plenty to say to me. My sister was pregnant and almost entirely wrapped up in her new household. My younger siblings now deemed me grown-up and had lost interest in me as a companion.

As I walked, more stars appeared.

I had written to Rufus who had not replied. I had written to Goode who had sent me a charcoal drawing of Salvador. She had invited me to visit but she had not mentioned Rufus.

I knew the constellations from the encyclopaedia.

Whenever I heard that the barge was in the basin, I went down to the Village quay. The barge master kept inviting me to join the barge. I was reluctant to leave the baby.

Ursus Major.

The barge master kept inviting me to Sing with her. On calm days, when the baby was in the Colony, the barge master and I would walk up to the head of the Loch and row out into mid-channel in an inflatable dingy. Once I got used to the dinghy's erratic movements, I could easily lose myself in Song with the barge master and the Loch.

Cassiopeia.

Occasionally, I took my father and the baby to visit the woman with the brand on her forehead. The woman was growing increasingly frail and liked to see her granddaughter.

Ursus Minor.

After a lot of prompting from the barge master, I rejoined the Village choir. The choir was in good voice and the choir teacher was hopeful of winning the Autumn Singing. I wondered who would be chosen by the oldest Wave Singer. The choir teacher said that there was a strong young Singer in the Settlement by the Loch.

Pegasus.

There was little enthusiasm in the Village for the Colonists' attempts to contact the satellite. The barge master said that it was unlikely that any of the satellite's systems still worked after such a long time. The choir teacher said that we had no means to harness microwave energy, even if we could restart the satellite.

Orion.

My father said that the satellites caused the Event. Further communication with them could only herald the Great Flood. Hark the herald angels sing, said my mother, braiding his long straggly hair into dreadlocks. Even if we could communicate with the satellite we wouldn't understand what it said.

Since the Event, the three stars in Orion's belt pointed north.

No one ever mentioned my finding my Stretch. No one ever mentioned my journey. No one ever mentioned The Project.

When I reached the Colony, the moon had risen. The centre of the Colony was lit with rush torches. A long trestle table stood outside the hut.

On the table were two clockwork radios joined back to back. Wired to the radios was a large metal frame full of oscillator circuits. Next to one end of the table was an eviscerated tumble dryer, with an umbilicus of twisted wires joining it to the frame. The exercise bicycle was linked with a broad leather belt to the pulley on the tumble dryer. Beside the other end of the table was a tall wooden tower, surmounted by a large dish, connected to the radios by a long cable.

The twin was bent over the table, fiddling with the assembly.

'So you've finished!' I said, lamely, to the twin.

'Come and have a look,' said the twin, straightening up.

'Where's the movement?' I asked.

'Built into the tumble dryer,' said the twin.

'Does it work?' I asked, foolishly.

'Of course it works!' said the twin.

The girl with red hair and large feet came out of the hut. Without acknowledging me, she began to climb the rope ladder up the side of the tower. Thinking of my father earthbound in his wheelchair, I anxiously watched her.

'What are you up to?' I asked.

'We're ready to try it all out,' said the twin.

'Right now?' I asked.

'Right now,' said the twin.

'I thought you only picked up the satellite at midday,' I said.

'We tried listening for it on and off through the day,' said the twin. 'It's overhead every couple of hours. And the signal's strongest at sunset.'

'What's she doing up there?' I asked.

'Adjusting the dish,' said the twin.

'So what do you want me to do?' I asked.

'Pedal of course!' said the twin. 'On you get.'

I climbed onto the exercise bike and tried to pedal. The pedals barely moved. I stood up and strained at the pedals.

'It feels really stiff,' I said, as the wheel began to turn.

'You're turning the drum as well as the dynamo,' said the twin. 'Get it up to around 20 kilometres per hour and hold it steady.'

As my rate of pedaling increased, the speedometer reading slowly climbed.

'It's almost time,' shouted the girl with red hair from the platform on top of the tower.

'How's the speed?' asked the twin.

I checked the speedometer.

'Just about there,' I said, pedaling furiously.
'Keep it steady,' said the twin. 'Here we go.'

The twin waved at the girl with red hair. The girl with red hair waved back. The twin threw a switch. A green light on the tumble dryer began to wink on and off in time with my pedaling.

The twin threw another switch and began to tune the radios. There was a short burst of static from the radios and then a low persistent hum.

'Keep going,' said the twin, hunched over the winking green light.

Suddenly, the satellite noise sounded from the radios.

As the green light winked, the twin threw a third switch.

The response from the disk played from the radios.

I looked at the twin, amazed.

'Keep going,' said the twin.

There was a short burst of satellite sounds that I hadn't heard before.

'Keep going,' said the twin again, *sotto voce*.

There was another short burst of satellite sounds and an unearthly voice said:

X-FLR6 Satellite 5 To Repeater Station 129.
Initiating Primary Startup Sequence.

Checking Core Systems.
Major Core Systems Failure.
Initiating Core Systems Repair.
Unable To Complete Core Systems Repair.

Initiating Backup Systems.
Major Backup Systems Failure.
Initiating Backup Systems Repair.
Unable to Complete Backup Systems Repair.

Primary Startup Sequence Complete.

Checking Ground Telemetry System.
Link With Repeater Station 129 Lost.

Initiating Power Startup Sequence. . .

And fell silent.

'What's happening?' I asked, still pedaling. 'What's happening?'

'It sounds like it's starting to generate power,' said the twin.

'But it can't!' I cried, stopping pedaling and getting off the exercise bike 'There's nowhere to receive the power! What'll happen if it tries to beam it back?'

'There'll probably be another Event,' said the twin, calmly.

'Look!' shouted the girl with red hair and large feet, pointing directly up at the sky above her. 'Look!'

A fourth star shone in Orion's belt. The star burnt brighter and brighter.

Everywhere I go

Facing page 8   John Berger & John Mohr,
A Seventh Man, Pelican, 1975, p229

Page 9, 95, 179, 253 West Coast Pop Art
Experimental Band, 'Outside/Inside', *Where's My
Daddy?*, Amos AA 7004, 1969

Page 98 Berthold Brecht, 'Motto', in *Brecht Poems
Part 2, 1929-1938*, Eyre Methuen, 1976, p321

Page 133 Berthold Brecht, 'Motto', in *Brecht Poems
Part 3, 1938-1956*, Eyre Methuen, 1976, p439

Chapter 1 first appeared in *Scottish Book Collector*,
Issue 7:2, December 2001, pp32-35

Kropotkin's birthday is 21st December.

Acknowledgements

I would like to thank my family and friends for their patience and encouragement during the long evolution of *The Wave Singer*. In particular, Ricky and Deb Howrie eagerly read each chapter, and Michael Grant, Catherine Jones, John Ophel and Alison Childs gave acute comments and suggestions.

I would especially like to thank: Wilma Alexander, for her painstaking checking of three major drafts; Jennie Renton, my first publisher, for her robust good sense; Derek Rodger of Argyll Publishing, for the precious gift of an ISBN.

Nancy Falchikov, my first, best critic, has lived with *The Wave Singer* since its inception. For love and Arkles, thank you!

Other Books from Argyll Publishing

www.argyllpublishing.com